A BOMBER'S NIGHT

A BOMBER'S NIGHT

PATSY ROMACK

Illustrated by

Kimberly Olmsted

for David & Ann -
thought you might like
to read my tribute to my mum & dad.
love
Patsy -

BLUFF HOUSE
Anchorage, Alaska

Acknowledgments

Without the encouragement and invaluable writing advice from Pam Cravez, this book would not have been written. Many, many thanks Pam.

Joyce Bamberger and Averil Lerman helped out at the start and finish; Darlene Dubay checked the final manuscript; Joanna Knapp gave publishing support. Thanks to all of you.

Jill Jameson and Enid Keill enriched the book with their wartime memories. Enid and Ian Keill took me to Bletchley Park to see the buildings where the Enigma codes were enciphered. They also took me to Cambridge where I was born and where the story unfolds.

Heartfelt thanks to my illustrator, Kim Olmsted. Her careful research of the time period and attention to detail made the characters and scenes come alive. -- PR

Library of Congress Control Number: 2009900118
Printed in the United States of America
Bluff House, Anchorage, Alaska

ISBN-13: 978-0-9820075-0-1

In memory of

Rita and Hans

Chapter 1

Cambridge, England – 1941

The moment she saw it, she knew. Jill's feet sank deeper into the soft dirt as she stared up at the sky. The dark shape drifting high above the trees was a Nazi bomber. Moonlight glinted off the fuselage and Jill saw something fall out of the plane.

Without stopping to water the rest of the vegetables, she grabbed her bucket and ran back to the house. Water spilled against her legs and dribbled into her shoes but Jill hardly noticed. As she reached for the back door knob she remembered her little sister down in the shed feeding Tuppence. She dropped the bucket and ran back through the yard.

"Een!" Jill pulled open the shed door. "We have to

go inside – now." She kept her voice slow and even.

"Why?" Enid barely looked up. She gathered a bundle of straw with the speed of a snail.

"Because…" Jill wanted to tell her sister about the plane, about the bomb she saw falling into the woods, but the war with Germany had made Enid very fearful. "Because it's bedtime," she said.

"I don't have to listen just because you're eleven." Enid drew herself up to her full height that, at seven years old, barely reached Jill's shoulder. She stuck her nose in the air and fine strands of blonde hair fell away from her face. Bits of dirt clung to her stubby fingers and there was mud on the hem of her skirt. Enid always looked as though she had just finished mucking out a barn. "I'm saying goodnight to Tuppence," she said importantly and continued to arrange straw around her pet tortoise.

Enid could be so infuriating. Beads of sweat gathered on Jill's scalp as she waited for her sister to finish. She distracted herself by making up a poem in her head.

"My little sister is a pill
She always does whate'er she will,
Why couldn't she be more like…"

"Me," thought Jill, debating whether or not another line might include the word "kill".

"Do hurry, Een." Jill wished for some of her mother's endless patience. She chewed on the side of her thumb, studied the torn, wet skin around the nail, then wiped it on her skirt. Her mother was always telling her to take her fingers out of her mouth.

Enid was still messing around with the straw when the siren went off, its hoarse wail screaming through the dark. Jill's stomach clenched and she plugged her fingers into her ears.

"Come on, Een!"

This time Enid listened. She snatched up Tuppence and grabbed Jill's hand as they ran from the shed. Searchlights swept the sky, their beams lighting rows of soft green cabbage leaves in the garden before rising up the brick walls, slate roofs and chimney stacks of the houses on Jill's street.

The back door of Jill's house opened. Her mother stepped out in her worn slippers and flowery apron and stood waiting by the tangle of honeysuckle. Jill piled into her arms, breathing in her mother's fresh gardenia soap smell. Enid squeezed in beside her.

"Oh, Mum, I could have died out there." Enid's voice reached a high soprano. She rolled her eyes dramatically. "I was settling Tuppence in the shed… and the siren went off… and it scared him… so I brought him in and…" She stopped to take a breath.

"And you're alright," said Mum quietly.

Jill followed her mother into the house, glad to be inside. She forgot about the plane in the sky and let her mother steer her towards the dining room.

Jill couldn't remember when they'd last had a meal in the dining room. Months ago, the table and chairs had

had to be replaced by the Morrison shelter, a giant metal cage with steel mesh sides, about the size of a double bed. Jill never liked seeing animals in cages, especially cramped ones, and every time she crawled inside the shelter she felt like an orangutan or a tiger at the London Zoo. Tonight she felt only fear at the thought of bombs dropping on the house and the dining room ceiling falling down on top of the shelter.

"Hurry up, Een," said Jill. Enid took her time getting to her place on the mattress, which filled the inside of the shelter.

"Goody. We don't have time to get into our pajamas," said Enid happily. Enid hated spending time getting in and out of clothes.

"I'm staying up here," Jill heard Charles call from the landing above. "I have some work to do."

Mum frowned.

Charles rented an upstairs room from Jill's parents and during air raids, he rarely used the shelter. Jill had heard him say he didn't have time and wondered what he had to do that was more important than taking shelter from bombs. She wanted him to be safe. On the rare occasions when he did join them, the shelter was much too cramped for comfort and Jill worried about Charles seeing her drool on her pillow when she fell asleep.

"Tom, where are you?" Mum called back into the hall.

"I'm here," said Dad, hurrying towards them with

a stack of medical files under his arm. He was a doctor at the university clinic. "I was gathering up work to pass the time." Dad pushed the files into the shelter, then folded up his lanky frame and came in after them. His fine blonde hair fell forward as he crawled. He brushed it away with a brown hand, tanned from playing tennis.

"If I read these files now, I'll be ready for the clinic tomorrow."

"But, Dad, tomorrow's Saturday," said Jill.

"I know dear. I have to go in anyway."

Jill smiled at her father. She admired how hard he worked and wondered if it helped distract him from the war. When he wasn't working, he played tennis. Maybe if she kept herself busier she wouldn't worry so much about reports of bombings on the radio and headlines of casualties in the newspaper. She decided she'd make a "to do" list.

Dad looked over at the dining room windows. "Did you check all the blackout curtains, Jill?"

"Yes, Dad, I did it after dinner," said Jill. "They're all closed up tight."

Jill knew that if light escaped around the edges of the curtains, their house would be seen from the sky. A speck of light could make not just their home but also their neighbours' houses enemy targets.

As Jill shifted around to get comfortable in the shelter she felt something hard beneath her.

"Hey, you're sitting on Tuppence!" Enid pummeled

Jill with her knees.

"I'll get off if you stop hitting me," Jill snapped back.

"If you had a shell like Tuppence, you wouldn't feel it."

Enid was forever comparing Tuppence to the rest of the world and he always came out ahead. During air raids everything about Enid was twice as irritating. Jill opened her mouth to grumble, but shut it when she saw Enid press her ear against the wire mesh to listen for planes. With a sigh, Jill pulled out the notebook she'd made with scraps of paper from her father's clinic and wrote,

"So what if Tuppence has a shell?

I don't need one – or his smell.

That little beast can go to …"

Jill paused before she wrote the last word. Her mother would make her vacuum all the carpets for a week if she caught her swearing. She wrote down "dwell" and "well" and lost interest in the poem. She began her "to do" list.

"Number one – remember to water vegetable garden before it gets dark."

Mum sat pinning up her hair into brown curls, while Dad unfolded himself beside Jill.

"I miss sleeping upstairs," said Jill.

On a clear night, from her bed upstairs she could see the moon above the trees. She could breathe the cool night air through the open window, and best of all, she could read under the covers in the dark with her flashlight. Downstairs in the Morrison shelter, it was stuffy and cramped and Enid's knees were everywhere. Jill hated the war.

"It's dangerous upstairs," said Enid in her important voice. "If a bomb hits us, we'd crash through the floor and wake up dead."

"That's stupid, Een," said Jill.

"Now, now girls," said Dad, propping himself up on his elbow. He barely fit the length of the shelter and he lay curved along the side like a long bracket. "I haven't heard anything about your day. Did anything interesting happen at school?"

Jill lay back on her pillow. Her breath evened out and her stomach began to unclamp. She liked telling her father about her school day.

"Something happened to me," said Enid, getting in first. "Emily White called me a Nazi lover and kicked me in the ankle." Enid's brown eyes grew moist and she sniffed. "See, I've got a bruise." She stuck her leg up into the narrow space above her head, pulling down her sock to reveal a small blue mark.

Jill studied the flowers on her pillow. Emily White and some of the other kids at school had also called her a "Nazi lover". It was because her family rented the living room to Lonnie and Fritz Muller and their baby Anna. They were refugees from Nazi Germany.

"I doubt that Lonnie and Fritz like the Nazis any more than Emily White does," said Dad, planting a kiss on Enid's bruise. "And we'll have to consider that bruise a 'war injury'."

"Are Lonnie and Fritz in their shelter?" asked Enid. A second Morrison shelter had been installed in the Muller's room for their safety.

"I'm sure they are, dear," said Mum.

"Fritz isn't a Nazi, is he Dad?" asked Enid.

"No, he isn't," said Dad.

"I like Fritz," said Enid. "Yesterday he showed me how to climb the apple tree and then he carried Anna up and she ate a leaf." Enid giggled.

"He's still a German," said Mum, scratching a rash on her hands. Tiny red spots spread from her fingers to her wrists. She suffered from allergic reactions to many things, like the lead in paint, and metal jewelry. She always scratched the rashes when she was upset. Jill wondered if she was allergic to Fritz.

"I like Fritz, Mum, now that I know him," said Jill. "And Lonnie. She helps me weed the garden."

"Fritz says he doesn't want to be German any more," said Enid.

Mum stayed quiet.

"After the war is over, Fritz says he and Lonnie will become British citizens," said Jill, thinking it would feel strange to adopt another country. She wouldn't want to.

"I hear a plane." Enid cocked her head sideways, listening.

Mum rested her hand on Enid's shoulder.

"It's far away. Don't think about it, dear." Mum lifted a tiny spider out of Enid's hair. "Look. A stowaway," she said, releasing the spider through the mesh of the shelter.

"Anything else happen at school, Enid?" asked Dad.

"Well…" said Enid. "Oh yes. Oliver Jones said his mum took tea and cookies to a German prisoner of war working in the fields at Fotherington Farm, and Emily White kicked Oliver, too."

"Tell her to kick sandbags instead of people," said Jill, remembering how her class had stacked a pile of them against the school walls to protect them from bomb blasts.

Dad turned to Jill.

"So what do you have to report, my dear?" he asked.

"Not much," said Jill. "Except that I couldn't concentrate at school."

"Why's that?"

"I was writing this poem in English class about my victory garden and the principal announced a practice air raid drill. I hate getting interrupted for stupid drills. We had to wear our gas masks, file out into the playground and climb down into the shelter. Then the teacher read all of our names and it took forever and when we got back to the classroom, writing was over."

"Who'd want to write a poem about vegetables?" asked Enid, wrinkling up her nose. "I'd write one about animals, like Tuppence."

"Not everybody eats, sleeps and breathes animals like you do, Een. Some of us are interested in other things, like plants and trees." Jill wanted to study botany when she went to college, and then she'd travel to far-off places and discover new plant forms. "Anyway Dad, you know how our gas masks look like they have snouts?" Dad nodded. "Well, when we walked out to the school shelter, Teddy Townsend said we looked like a crowd scene in a Mickey Mouse cartoon and got put in the corner for making squeaking noises."

Dad laughed.

"Then at recess he called me 'Minnie Mouse' and said, 'Who cares about poison gas anyway.'"

"Well, he needs to care," said Dad. "We all do."

"I think he acts silly because he's scared. His Dad's

off fighting in Germany," said Jill, studying some dirt under her thumbnail. Then she remembered. "I saw a plane above the woods before the siren went off."

"It could have been an owl," said Enid, the expert on every bird and beast that ever lived. "Barn owls drift into trees."

"It could have been a Royal Air Force helicopter out reconnoitering," said Mum. "The airfield is just beyond the woods."

"I think it was an owl," said Enid.

Enid always had to have the last word.

"If I have time we'll walk through the woods tomorrow and take a look," said Dad. "Isn't it time for a dragon story?"

"Ooh yes, Dad." Enid clapped her hands. "Last night Molly and Maisie went to look for the dragon in the cellar under the university clinic."

"And," continued Jill, "his fiery breath scorched Molly's math homework and the teacher said, 'I've heard a few stories in my day but this one takes the cake.'"

Dad cleared his throat.

"So, where were we?" he said. "Ah yes. Molly and Maisie decided to end the dragon's rule of terror. Molly had read that even the fiercest dragon would melt into a disgusting pool of purple jelly when sprayed with soapy water. Taking a full bottle of Lux detergent and a nine-foot length of garden hose, they snuck out of the house at midnight and rode their bikes down to the iron gates of Christ's College..."

A faint buzz sounded above the house.

"Dad, I hear another plane." Jill pressed closer to her mother.

A dull thud shook the dining room walls and bits of plaster fell onto the carpet. Enid whimpered and curled into a ball.

"It's alright, Een." Jill forgot to be irritated at her sister and tried to sound calm, like her mother. "Look. Tuppence doesn't mind the noise. He's nibbling on my blouse."

Out in the hall the phone rang.

"We don't have to answer," said Mum.

"It might be the fire hall," said Dad. "I should get it."

Dad raised himself to his knees, backed out of the shelter and walked into the hall.

Jill listened to her father talking on the phone and hoped it wasn't the fire hall. It wasn't fair, she thought. All day long her father was busy being a doctor. Why did he need to volunteer at night too? It frightened Jill when her father left during an air raid. She knew how the fire bombs fell first and lit up the sky so the enemy could see where to drop the explosives. Fighting fires put her father in the middle of danger. Her friend Alice's father had been badly burned when he'd volunteered. He'd had to stay in the hospital for ages and when he came out he looked different. Jill saw him at the school bazaar and he had patches of ugly red skin on his face and hands.

When Dad came back from the phone, he pulled on his thick wool fireman's pants and reached for his jacket. Jill saw the buttons glint in the dark as he fastened them one by one.

"I have to go," he said, slipping his belt around his waist and adjusting the axe which hung from it.

"I don't want you to," whispered Enid. "You'll get killed."

"I'll be careful, sweetheart, I promise."

Dad leaned into the shelter and hugged Enid. Jill reached her arms around her father's neck and fought back the tears. The house always felt so empty when he left. She thought about the plane she had seen and imagined dozens more flying across the English Channel towards them. She was glad her father wasn't fighting in Germany, but that didn't make him safe.

"Now don't you worry," said Dad. "If you're awake when I get back, I'll tell you what happened to the dragon."

Jill watched her mother hold her father's face between her hands and kiss him quickly before he strapped his helmet on his head and was gone.

Chapter 2

Jill awoke to the clip clop of Eddie's horse pulling the milk-cart up the street. The clock on the dresser said 8:15. Eddie was late.

Beside her in the Morrison shelter, Enid twitched in her sleep, murmuring something about Tuppence. Jill hoped it was a happy dream. These days her own dreams often held troubling visions of poison gas seeping into the house, misplaced gas masks and walls crumbling down around her. The morning sun cast fish net lines over Enid's cheek through the metal mesh of the shelter's sides. Seeing her parents were up, Jill backed quietly out of the shelter and pulled on her clothes. She remembered the air raid last night and wondered whose house had been hit.

"This is the BBC Home Service," announced the

radio as Jill entered the kitchen. She kissed her mother's cheek.

"Eddie's late with the milk, Mum," she said.

"I know, dear." Mum smiled. "I can't imagine why."

Most mornings, Jill could set the clock by Eddie. He'd only been late twice before – the morning his son Peter had had an emergency appendectomy and the day his horse took a walk in a neighbouring field and ended up in Mrs. Gibbons's orchard. Jill liked Eddie. He was always kind and friendly and often asked her about her victory garden. She promised to give him some cabbages when they were fully grown. Even though he called her "Jilly", he sometimes let her ride along with him and help deliver the milk.

Lonnie sat at the kitchen table, spooning oatmeal into six-month-old Anna's mouth.

"Where's Fritz?" asked Jill, walking past Lonnie to get the milk jug.

"He sleeps. Last evening he is helping so much Eddie with the milk accounts and then all night he has air raid patrol."

Anna's sticky hand grabbed at Lonnie's sleeve.

"Ach, Annachen, always you make messes on my sweaters." Lonnie picked a lump of oatmeal off her sleeve.

"You finished your new sweater, Lonnie," said Jill, pulling the milk jug off the shelf. "I really like it."

Jill loved everything about Lonnie – the arch of her eyebrows, the stylish fit of her clothes and the way her hair hung in loose waves. Jill's tight curls stuck out at odd angles, as did her eyebrows, and every weekday she had to wear her disgustingly ugly school uniform. In addition to looking perfect, Lonnie had a green thumb. When Jill's father was too busy, Lonnie helped Jill turn the soil and dig up weeds in the vegetable garden. She never got hot and sweaty.

"Thank you," said Lonnie, looking pleased. "Just last night I sew the sweater pieces together."

"You're such a good knitter, Lonnie," said Jill.

"Why don't you join one of those groups that knit socks for soldiers," said Mum. "They're always looking for good knitters."

"I ask them already once," said Lonnie, "but the woman she says 'no thank you' because... because I'm German."

"Oh," said Mum.

"That's mean," said Jill, unsure if her mother thought so too.

Lonnie wedged another spoon of porridge into Anna's mouth. The baby waved her arms and blew onto the spoon. Bits of porridge spattered onto her fat cheeks and dribbled down her chin.

"I'd better get the milk," said Jill, walking towards the back door.

"Be careful in the street, dear," called Mum. Jill was glad her mother let her go about her business as usual even after an air raid. It made the day seem more normal and the war a little less frightening. She'd seen Emily White's mother get all hysterical about a bomb raid as far away as London and Emily had dark circles around her eyes because she had trouble getting to sleep.

"I'll be careful," said Jill.

She opened the door and walked outside. Grey dust blew up around her shoes and the air smelled like firecrackers on Guy Fawkes Night. A plume of black smoke blew over the rooftops, swirled down the street and shouldered into the fronts of the houses. Jill thought the bomb must have hit the next street over.

Eddie's horse didn't care about the smoke. He stood by the curb as usual, his head halfway into a bag of food. Jill could hear his teeth grinding the grain. A man leaned against the side of the milk cart, his arms folded across a white apron. It wasn't Eddie.

"Hurry up," he said gruffly. "I haven't got all day."

"Where's Eddie?" asked Jill.

"He won't be coming." The man snapped out the words. Jill wanted to ask why but she just stared helplessly until the man said, "His house was hit. He's in hospital. Now hold out your jug."

Grasping a milk churn on the cart, the man tipped it forward. A funnel of milk arced into Jill's jug.

Jill tightened her grip and tried to focus on the stream of milk, but the edges went blurry and trying not to cry made her throat hurt. She drew in a lungful of smoky air, not wanting to believe that Eddie was hurt. He had brought the milk as long as she could remember. Last summer, when Eddie had taken their class to the dairy, his son Peter had squirted milk in her eye. She wondered if Peter was all right. The jug shook in Jill's hand, spilling milk on the path.

"Hey." The man's voice cut into Jill's thoughts and she felt his hand on her shoulder. "They're good at the hospital. They'll patch him up." His face had softened slightly.

Jill hurried back into the house where Mum sat at the kitchen table, sipping her morning tea.

"Oh Mum," sobbed Jill, dumping the milk jug in front of her mother, "Eddie's house was hit and he's in the hospital."

Mum pulled Jill into her lap, smoothed her hair and wiped her tears with the corner of her apron.

"And... Mum," Jill squeezed the corners of her eyes, trying to hold the tears back. "Peter and his mum might be hurt, too."

Jill noticed the untouched newspaper lying by her father's plate.

"Where's Dad?"

"He isn't home yet," said Mum. "When I called the fire hall the men were still out working. I'll call again after breakfast. I need your help, dear." She lit the burner under a pot of water.

"When the water boils, add enough porridge for you and Enid."

Jill took the spoon from her mother, stirring in the porridge when the water boiled. Thinking about her father, she watched the lumpy mass heave and belch like molten lava. She wanted to see her father now. Waiting for him was the hardest thing in the world.

The longest he'd ever been gone was when a German bomber pilot had crashed into the fields. He'd taken the pilot to the hospital and Jill had overheard her mother asking him about it later. "It was terrible, dear," Jill had heard and then he shut the door, so she couldn't hear the rest. Somewhere south of London, there was a hospital for burn victims. Jill had read about it.

What if a floor collapsed under her father and he fell into a fire? Jill shivered in spite of the steam rising up from the porridge. She could barely remember back to before the war, when the worst thing in her life had been catching the whooping cough, and she'd coughed so hard she'd almost heaved out her lungs on the sidewalk.

"Yuck," said Enid, coming into the kitchen with her hand over her nose. "I hate porridge. It smells like chicken poop. Why can't we have eggs and bacon?"

"Enid, please," said Mum.

Enid hated it when they ran out of bacon coupons in their ration book, but Jill missed bananas the most. They never had those anymore. Jill longed for their smooth sweetness. Before the war she'd had one for breakfast every morning.

"Where's Dad?" asked Enid.

"He's out," said Jill. Usually Enid wasn't satisfied with a simple answer but today she sat down next to Lonnie.

"Is Fritz asleep?"

"Yes." Lonnie lifted Anna out of the high chair and sat her on her lap. "He is all night out on air raid patrol."

"I wish we never, ever had air raids."

"You're full of wishes," said Mum.

An airmail letter marked with ink stamps lay on the table.

"Is that from Germany?" asked Enid.

"Yes," said Lonnie.

"What's this say?" Enid pointed to some printed words.

"That the letter passed the censors," said Lonnie.

"What are censors?" Enid looked confused.

"The censors check information coming in from Germany," said Mum. "If they read anything suspicious, they report it to the War Office."

"What could possibly be suspicious about a letter

Lonnie got from her parents?" asked Jill, wondering if her mother felt suspicious of Lonnie.

Mum examined one of the larger spots on her wrist.

"I don't know, dear," she said. "But that's what the censors have to do."

"I wouldn't want anyone reading my letters," said Enid.

"I am happy just to hear from my parents." Lonnie and her parents were Jewish and everyone knew that the Nazis hated Jews. "I wish they could leave Berlin and come to England. But they cannot get passports."

Waiting for Dad is hard enough, thought Jill, but Lonnie's father was in Germany and she had to wait endlessly for news of him, her mother and her other relatives left behind in Germany.

Anna made small grunting sounds and her face turned red.

"Anna's pooing." Enid pushed back her chair and flung her hand across her nose. "Phew, it smells worse than porridge!"

"Come, Anna." Lonnie lifted the baby out of the high chair and hurried out of the room.

"Een, you have less tact than a mouse. Couldn't you see that Lonnie was missing her parents?"

Enid hung her head over her bowl. The milk had seeped under her porridge and the grey mass rose from the bottom of the bowl like a submarine rising out of the ocean. Jill wanted to tell her it was time for a spoonful of cod liver oil. Enid hated cod liver oil even more than porridge, but before she could say anything, Charles walked in. Jill was relieved to see that once again he had survived the night up in his room. He wore his old tweed jacket with pockets that sagged below the hemline. Jill often wondered what on earth he kept in them.

"Here," said Charles holding out a magazine to Jill. "You left this in the bathroom."

Jill blushed bright red. Today of all days, she didn't want Charles to notice her. Somehow she always made an enormous fool of herself around him but yesterday had been unimaginable. She'd forgotten to lock the bathroom door and Charles had walked in on her, sitting on the toilet with her pants around her ankles, reading *A Gardener's Guide to Healthy Vegetables.* She'd wanted to flush herself down the pipes and be gone forever.

Jill reached for the magazine, trying to keep her face hidden behind the milk jug.

"Thanks," she said.

"Sorry to bother you, Peggy, but I can't find any socks." He smiled at Mum, pushing his glasses up his nose. Charles could never keep track of his clothes, even though Mum washed, ironed and put them away for him. Jill often sorted and stowed Charles's socks. She suspected he had some up in his drawer and had simply forgotten.

"There are some in that basket." Mum pointed to

the floor.

"Thank you." Charles looked into the basket. He picked up a plaid pair and stuffed them into one of the sagging pockets. "Is Tom in? I was going to help him mend some light fuses before I went over to the university." Charles taught mathematics at Christ's College.

"He's not back yet," said Mum, scratching her rash.

"Is he at the clinic?" asked Charles.

"No, he's still at the bomb site."

"Ah," said Charles. "I'll be upstairs for a while."

The doorbell rang and before Mum could stop her, Enid ran down the hall to see who it was. A few moments later Jill heard Tante Marlene's German accent echo in the hallway. Tante Marlene was Fritz's older sister. She had helped Fritz and Lonnie get out of Germany. Her English husband, Doctor Harry Richards, worked at the clinic with Jill's father. When Harry asked if Fritz and Lonnie could stay at Jill's house, Mum had bristled because they were German, but Dad had insisted they come.

"I bring sugar for our coffee," Tante Marlene was saying, "and for you, Enid, there is plenty to make your porridge sweet." Tante Marlene often shared her rations with Lonnie and Fritz, because aliens were not allowed to have ration books.

Tante Marlene entered the kitchen and plumped herself down onto a chair. Her cheeks were flushed almost as red as her hair, which Lonnie had told Jill was not natural like Fritz's, but dyed with henna. Lonnie knew about stuff like that.

"Good morning, Mum. Good morning, Jill."

Taking out a pack of cigarettes, Tante Marlene selected one, placed it into a cigarette holder and lit it.

"Ah," she said with satisfaction. The white ruffles over her bosom rose and fell as she drew in the smoke. Below the ruffles flowed a deep red, polka dotted silk skirt and below that, nylons and red high-heeled shoes.

Tante Marlene always dressed as if the king had invited her to visit him at Buckingham Palace. Should Tante Marlene ever be invited, Jill planned to go with her. The cigarette holder added to the glamour. Enid didn't seem to notice that the holder was made of fine tortoise shell.

Mum liked Tante Marlene, even though she was German. Maybe being married to an Englishman made her seem less German, Jill thought. Tante Marlene was so kind and friendly, it was difficult not to like her.

"I come to help Lonnie with my little Anna."

"Lonnie went to change Anna's diaper," said Mum. "Can I make you some breakfast, Marlene?"

"No, no, Peggy dear." Tante Marlene patted her stomach. "You sit down and drink your tea. You are not sleeping much, I think, last night."

"No," Mum agreed. "It was a long night." Mum fiddled at her neck with the gold chain Dad had given her. "Will Harry cover for Tom at the clinic today… if…

if Tom can't go?"

Tante Marlene took Mum's hand and squeezed it.

"Yes, of course. He tells me he goes later this afternoon. This morning he is making the house calls."

Lonnie came back into the kitchen and Tante Marlene held out her arms for Anna.

"Come, liebling."

Anna danced her legs up and down on Tante Marlene's skirt. The silky material slid between Tante Marlene's legs, revealing the tip of a garter where it attached to a stocking. It would be a long time before Jill could wear nylon stockings, especially since they were scarce in the war. She wondered how anyone ever kept the seams straight. When a girl down the street didn't have stockings, she just painted black lines down the backs of her legs.

Anna reached for the cigarette in Tante Marlene's mouth.

"Ach, no you don't," said Tante Marlene, turning her head away. Ashes fell amongst the ruffles of her blouse and she tried to brush them out. "Here, Lonnie – you take this little rascal so I can get the sugar for Enid's porridge."

"You mustn't beg for sugar, Enid." Mum frowned.

"No Peggy, she didn't beg." Tante Marlene pinched Enid's cheek affectionately. "Enid, she is my good girl." She dug deep into her bag. "Here is some jam for your toast, Peggy, and here are some German magazines for you, Lonnie. I have to stop Harry from throwing them out."

"Well, Marlene, if you wouldn't mind keeping an eye on things," Mum stood up, "I'll go next door for a minute."

"Yes, of course you go, Peggy. While you are gone, we do the dishes, Lonnie and I."

"Thank you," said Mum and walked into the hall to get her handbag.

When Mum had gone, Jill offered to help with the dishes.

"You are a good girl too, Jill," said Tante Marlene. "Just like Lonnie when she is a girl."

"You knew Lonnie when she was my age?"

"Yes." Tante Marlene rolled up her sleeves. "She lives close by in Berlin. Always she comes to the park when I take Fritz and his friends roller skating."

"Didn't you mind watching the little kids?" Jill hated how Enid wanted to tag along every time she did anything.

"Not at all. I loved it. Almost I feel like a mother to Fritz – I am much older by seventeen years."

Jill couldn't imagine feeling like a mother to Enid. She thought that someday she could be a mother to a baby like Anna.

"Lonnie's a good mother," said Jill.

"I try to be," said Lonnie and then she got quiet.

"What is wrong?" asked Tante Marlene.

"Well, yesterday I am at the store and a woman she said to me how beautiful Anna is and when I said thank you, she hears my voice and turns to her friend and says, 'Too bad her mother is a German.' Lonnie wiped a tear from the corner of her eye.

"Anna's the luckiest baby in the world to have you as a mum," said Jill. "And I'm glad you're living with us. It's been two whole months today since you came."

"I know." Lonnie managed a smile. "And two whole months since Fritz came back." When the war began, the government had suspected all German refugees of being spies and had put them in internment camps on the Isle of Man. Fritz had been held for a year but Lonnie wasn't allowed to go because she was pregnant. So she stayed with Tante Marlene and Harry.

"We squeezed a cot in when Anna was born," said Tante Marlene, "and we would have taken Fritzchen too, but he said his family is too big for our small flat, now with Anna."

Jill finished the dishes and got her notebook out of the Morrison shelter. Then she went into the hall and sat on the stairs to wait for her father. She opened her notebook and added "Help Dad with his filing" to her list. Enid came out and began shifting a pile of books around the floor.

"I'm going to build a maze for Tuppence. Hold him for me, Jill, please."

Enid stood the books up for walls and added some lettuce leaves at the far end for bait. When she placed Tuppence at the entrance to the maze, he didn't move.

"Come on Tuppence," said Enid. "Find the food."

Tuppence sniffed the air and tentatively reached out a scaly leg. It hit the nearest book, which hit another and another and Enid watched the entire maze flattened like a row of dominoes.

"Give up, Een. He'll never be Einstein."

"Yes, he will. In fact, I've just read," said Enid, drawing herself up importantly, "that wood turtles can learn to run a maze almost as quickly as rats."

"That doesn't prove anything. Tuppence isn't a wood turtle and I have yet to see him run anywhere."

Ignoring Jill, Enid flopped down and began reconstructing the maze.

Fritz came into the hall, looking sleepy with the cord of his robe trailing along the floor. He had a slight build and wasn't quite as tall as Jill's father, but he did push-ups every morning and he could ride circles around Jill on his bike.

Dark stubble covered his chin and a wedge of red hair stuck up from his head like a rooster's comb. Mumbling good morning, he sat down next to Jill and scratched his scalp vigorously as if to get the blood flowing through his brain.

"Every morning when I wake up, I am happy to be free and I am with Lonnie."

Jill smiled at Fritz but stayed quiet.

"You are waiting for someone, yes?"

"For Dad," said Jill. "Fritz, when you were out last night, did you see him?" During air raids, Fritz did air raid patrol duty, checking houses for specks of light and teaching people how to use stirrup pumps. Thinking hard, Fritz rubbed his chin.

"I see fire trucks, but I did not see your father. Putting out flames, it takes time." Fritz patted Jill's knee. "Soon your father he comes."

Fritz turned his attention to Enid sitting amid the books on the floor.

"Enid, I see already you and Tuppence have been reading many books." He grinned mischievously.

Enid scowled and kicked at the fallen books.

"Please Enid, I make only a joke. Let me help with your maze. I am good with building books. Not long ago I am a boy who likes to play with trains."

At twenty-nine, it seemed to Jill that Fritz was a long way from boyhood.

"The books," he said, "you can stick them like this."

Enid watched as Fritz made piles of books, three high.

"You mean – stack not stick." Enid giggled, falling back off her heels and almost kicking Tuppence with her foot.

"You stack, I stick," said Fritz, winking at Jill. She

thought Enid rude for laughing at Fritz's English. Fritz had told Jill that some people objected to him being a fire warden when they heard his accent. He was so kind and gentle, Jill couldn't bear the thought. She knew what it felt like to be laughed at. Emily White had laughed at her for saying "a-genius" instead of "indigenous" once when she read out loud at school. "You're no genius," Emily had snickered.

Now that he could see a clear path, Tuppence crept towards the lettuce leaves. When he was halfway there, Lonnie and Tante Marlene came into the hall with Anna and sat her on the floor. Anna saw Tuppence and flapped her arms like a bird taking flight.

Tuppence pulled in his head and legs, sealed tight like an army tank awaiting attack.

"Phooey," said Enid. "He'll never come out now."

But no one was listening. They were watching Anna pump herself towards Tuppence, her hands and knees slapping the floor.

"Anna, look at you!" Fritz clapped his hands. "You learn to crawl."

"Hurrah, Anna." Jill dropped to her knees and followed Anna down the hall. When they reached the front door, Jill heard the key turned in the lock.

"Whoa, Anna." Jill grabbed the baby.

The door opened and Mum stood grey-faced before them, scratching at the rash on her arms.

"Mum, what's wrong?" Jill passed Anna to Lonnie.

"Eddie's wife and Peter are safe but no one at the fire has seen your father."

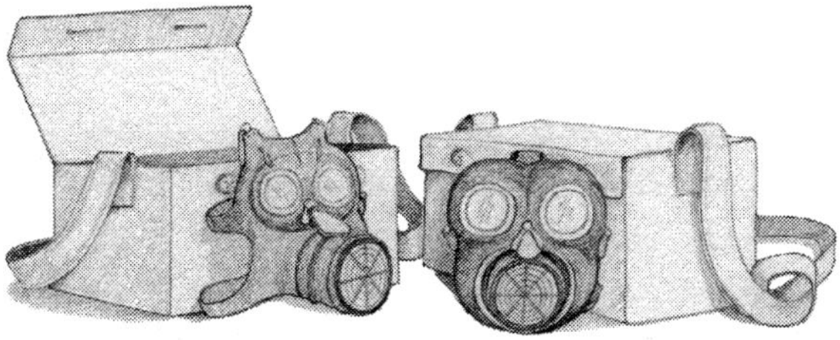

Chapter 3

Enid forgot all about Tuppence and ran to Mum. "Where's Dad!" she sobbed. "I want him."

"So do I, dear," said Mum, pulling her close.

Jill wondered why no one had seen her father at the fire. Had the smoke been too thick? Had he gone in looking for Eddie and been crushed by falling masonry? Was he dead? Jill didn't have any answers.

"I go to the fire hall and see if I can help," said Fritz.

"No," said Mum, not looking at Fritz. "There's nothing you can do."

Fritz looked hurt when he left the room. Tante Marlene stepped forward.

"Peggy." She touched Mum's arm. "Fritz, he is a good boy. He wants to help. And you are tired. Please let me to stay. I can make telephone calls."

Mum looked down at the floor and Jill couldn't tell if she was crying.

"Thank you, Marlene. I could use that kind of help."

Mum wrote down some names and numbers for Tante Marlene.

Jill heard a door open upstairs and Charles came down.

"Is Tom back yet?" He shifted from one foot to the other, the toe of an argyle sock poking through a hole in his slipper.

"No," said Mum.

"Can I do anything to help?" offered Charles.

Mum shook her head no.

"I'm off to the university, then," said Charles. "I'll be back soon."

After Charles left, Jill noticed the stack of her father's medical files on the hall table, the ones he'd been working on in the Morrison shelter before the siren went off last night.

"Mum, I could take Dad's files to the clinic," she offered. "They might need them."

Mum ran her fingers through her hair and gathered in her breath. "I suppose so."

"Here's Dad's briefcase." Jill held it open and Mum put the files inside.

"Can I come too?" asked Enid.

"You'll dawdle around looking for bugs and things," said Jill. "And I'll be hanging around waiting for you."

"I won't either!" Enid crossed her arms and poked out her chin. "I'll keep up this time, I promise."

"Oh, all right," said Jill, remembering how her father always asked her to be kind to her sister.

She snatched up her gas mask and handed Enid hers.

"Be careful," said Mum as she kissed them goodbye.

Jill and Enid walked down to the shed to get their bikes. Fritz stood outside the shed with his bike upside down against the fence. He was trying to spin the back wheel, but it appeared to be stuck. He kicked the frame.

"Scheisse!"

"Are you swearing, Fritz?" asked Jill, wheeling her bike out of the shed.

Fritz looked sheepish.

"This stupid bike it never works. I had one so excellent back home."

"Why didn't you bring it?" asked Enid.

"I cannot bring my things. I leave in such a hurry Berlin."

"Did the Nazis chase you?" asked Enid.

"Don't be silly, Een," said Jill, even though she thought they might well have. Lonnie had told her how much the Nazis had frightened her. They wouldn't let Jews go in some stores or sit on certain park benches. Jill didn't think she'd like living in a country where there were laws about where you could sit and who you were allowed to see, with Nazis watching you all the time in case you made a mistake. Lonnie also said that she and Fritz had to meet in secret in Berlin, because she was Jewish. When the Nazis found out, they came to get him and put him in jail. Fortunately, a good attorney got him out.

"When Lonnie and I leave Germany, we fooled the Nazis." Fritz smiled. "We did not travel together but when we got to England we met and got married."

"Are the Nazis still after you?" Enid glanced behind to see if there were Nazis hiding in the hedges along the back lane. Fritz laughed.

"I hope not."

"Come on, Een. We have to go," said Jill. "Good luck with your bike, Fritz."

Lilacs tumbled over hedgerows and Jill inhaled their scent as she and Enid rode their bikes over the ruts in the lane. Enid stopped every few seconds to look over her shoulder.

"What are you doing?" asked Jill.

"Looking for Nazis," she said, bumping over a clump of grass.

"Don't be silly, Een. There aren't any Nazis here."

"Well, there are some in the fields near Granchester. Mum and I saw them from the bus."

"Those men are prisoners of war, Een."

"Mum says they are German boys like Fritz, but I said Fritz is different."

"I've seen them out there working, too," said Jill. "They look just like the other farm hands."

"What if one escaped?" Enid looked back again.

"You'd probably walk right by him without even noticing."

They reached the street and walked past the anti-aircraft tank parked on the corner. The tanks sat on Cambridge street corners in case of an air raid. Jill hadn't ever seen this one shoot at anything and it certainly hadn't prevented a bomb from being dropped on Eddie's house. When they came to the short cut through the woods, Jill steered her bike towards it. The path wound its way through a stand of oak and sycamore trees.

Jill loved the quietness of the woods. She wished she could stop and look for bluebells or let Enid gather up beetles and spiders for her "scientific investigations", as she called them.

Up ahead, two sniffing Jack Russell terriers pulled a small woman in large Wellington boots along the path.

As Enid rode by, the dogs stopped to bark at her bike basket. She swerved, lost her balance and landed in a small bush. A bundled up towel fell out of the basket onto the ground.

The woman struggled to pull the dogs away.

"Rufus! Rosy! No!" she scolded. "Are you all right, dear?" she called back to Enid as the dogs dragged her off.

Jill frowned at her sister.

"Een, you didn't, did you?"

Enid picked up the towel bundle and Tuppence poked his head out of the folds.

"So what if I brought Tuppence? You didn't say I couldn't. Those dogs scared him and now he's going to pee. If he wets his towel, he'll catch a cold. Remember – he's ectothermic."

Jill rolled her eyes. Enid threw out scientific terms just to annoy her.

"I don't need a speech about categories of cold-blooded animals," said Jill, thinking about snakes and lizards and other creepy things. She shivered at the thought. She could never love a tortoise like her sister could. "Tell Tuppence you promised not to hold me up."

"He'll be quick." Enid took Tuppence off towards a patch of dirt.

Jill leaned against the trunk of a sycamore and squinted up at the sky. A hawk flew high above the leaves and a few small clouds drifted into view. Breathing in the damp forest smell, she remembered how frightening the sky had seemed last night and a serious poem began to form.

"I fear the danger of the night,
But not the blue of morning light
It lifts me up just like a…"

Jill giggled. She thought of *Winnie the Pooh* in Enid's favourite story, when Pooh is lifted by a balloon and hopes the bees will mistake him for a cloud. She was wondering how it would feel to be chased by a swarm of bees, when something tickly landed on her neck.

"Eeek!" screamed Jill.

Enid came running over to see what had happened.

"There's something on my neck," shrieked Jill. "Get it off, Een." Jill turned her neck towards Enid. "Get it off now!"

"It's just a spider, Jill."

Jill felt Enid's hands scoop the spider off her neck and turned to see her sister examining it with interest.

"I don't know how you can you touch those things, Een. They're gross."

"You might say 'thank you'." Enid hung the spider on a nearby leaf.

"Thank you, Een. I owe you for that." Jill brushed at her neck to be sure no spider webbing lurked there. "We'd better go. Where's Tuppence?"

Enid walked to where she'd left Tuppence. After a

few seconds she called back to Jill in a panicky voice.

"I can't find Tuppence. He's gone."

Jill came over to where Enid crouched, frantically scanning the greenery around her.

"Of course he isn't gone, silly. At a quarter of a mile an hour, he's hardly going to make it across a leaf. He's probably napping in the bushes."

"Tuppence! Tuppence!" Enid yelled.

"That's not going to do any good, is it?"

"It might," said Enid. "He knows my voice and he looks right at me when I say hello."

Jill dropped down beside her sister. Broken branches littered the ground, pressing into her knees as she crawled into the nearest bush. The strap of her gas mask snagged on a branch. Darn! Why did she have to carry this stupid gas mask everywhere she went? She stopped to untangle it and wondered if children in Germany had to wear gas masks. Then she wondered if Jewish children in Germany were allowed to wear them, since the rules were different for the Jews. She'd have to ask Lonnie.

The earth smelled of rain and mulch and she felt the presence of more long-legged insects hanging above her, just waiting to drop into her clothes.

"Een, you'd better be looking," she called over her shoulder.

Furry things brushed up against her forehead as Jill moved further into the bushes. Tentatively, she felt the ground around her, expecting to feel a bunch of squishy slugs but hoping to feel Tuppence's cool shell. Then she felt something quite unexpected, something soft and silky. Pulling it towards her, Jill backed out of the bushes. She kept on pulling until a huge pile of material lay before her on the ground.

Enid came up with Tuppence in her arms.

"What's that?" Enid pointed at the material.

"A parachute," said Jill. "I saw a plane above the trees last night, and now I'm thinking someone parachuted out of it."

Enid rubbed her hand over the silky material then abruptly pulled back.

"It's Nazis, isn't it?" she said. "They're coming after Fritz."

"No, silly. But it could be a fifth columnist."

"A what?"

"A fifth columnist. You know, Een, like what the government thought Fritz was when he was sent to the Isle of Man. They think a fifth army column has been dropped in by parachute near Cambridge."

Enid backed away, gripping Tuppence to her chest. "Let's get out of here."

Jill stuffed the parachute back in the bushes.

"Een, you can't tell a soul about this, promise?"

"I promise, I promise. Just come on!"

Jill stood up and brushed bits of dirt and leaves from her skirt, then scrambled out to the path where Enid had already settled Tuppence into her bike basket.

When they got to Christ's College, Tante Marlene's car pulled up alongside them. She lowered the window.

"Hello, my dears. It is a good thing I see you again. I make cookies and forget to give them to you."

Tante Marlene opened the car door and eased herself onto the sidewalk. She held two paper bags, one in each hand.

"These are the cookies and this is Harry's lunch. I tell him I leave it for him at the clinic for when he comes in at noon."

"I'm taking Dad's files in," said Jill. "I can put Harry's lunch on his desk."

"How kind of you, Jill. I go then to the library and return my books."

Jill and Enid pushed their bikes into the crowded rack outside the college. Two students came out of the building, their black gowns hanging low off their shoulders.

"I'm not going to university if I have to study on Saturdays," said Enid, watching the students load their bikes with books.

"That means you can't be a veterinary doctor."

"Yes I can." Enid always had an answer. "I'll study during the week. Anyway, I'm like a plant, I learn by osmosis – my teacher said so."

Jill thought it would be a vast improvement if Enid was a plant. Plants were easy to get along with.

"I'm going into the clinic, Een. Are you coming?"

"I'll stay here by the bike rack with Tuppence," said Enid, eyeing a patch of grass in front of her. "I'll watch him, I promise."

"O.K. I won't be long."

As Jill crossed the path towards the clinic she saw Charles on the far side of the quadrangle. He waved at Jill, almost dropping a box he was carrying. Jill wondered if he dropped the chalk when he wrote math formulas on the board during class and if his students laughed at him for being clumsy. She hoped they didn't.

When she entered the clinic, Jill poked her head around the door but Mrs. Hopkins, the secretary, wasn't at her desk. The room smelled of disinfectant and on the radio, Vera Lynn's voice crooned "There'll be blue birds over, the white cliffs of Dover".

Jill walked past the reception desk and put Harry's lunch on his desk. Around the corner stood her father's desk. Dad smiled out of a picture taken last Christmas with the whole family standing under the mistletoe. Jill sat down in Dad's chair and ran her finger over the metal frame.

A noise startled her and she jumped up and went into the hall, where a string of weak bulbs cast dim pools of light along the floor.

"Mrs. Hopkins?" she called. When no one answered she walked down the hall. She stopped at the steps leading down into the cellar where all the files were kept.

"Mrs. Hopkins," she called again. No one answered.

Jill climbed down the stone steps, brushing cobwebs from her face. A beetle scurried into a crack in the wall. She shivered. Down here, creepy things lurked in every shadow and Jill suspected that skeletons lay buried in the walls. She avoided the college cellar whenever she could and barely tolerated the thought of it in Dad's bedtime stories. Strange creatures seemed to lurk in every corner.

When Jill reached the bottom of the steps, she saw Mrs. Hopkins reaching for files on a far shelf.

"Mrs. Hopkins."

"Goodness me!" Mrs. Hopkins jumped. A small cloud of dust flurried around her ankles. She turned to Jill and peered at her over the top of her reading glasses. A few strands of white hair had escaped her bun and hung in wisps by her ears.

"You surprised me dear. What can I do for you?"

"Dad finished these files at home last night and he would have brought them in today, only..." Jill trailed off.

Mrs. Hopkins took the files and placed her hand gently on Jill's arm.

"Only he couldn't." Mrs. Hopkins finished Jill's sentence and looked at her with soft hazel eyes. A maze of lines etched the skin around them. Jill swallowed hard.

"Dad went to fight fires last night and he hasn't come home yet." She concentrated on the rows of shelves disappearing into the gloom. If Mrs. Hopkins hugged her now, she knew she'd cry.

"I see," she said, looking at Jill for a long minute.

Mrs. Hopkins had known Dad since before Jill's birth. She always told Jill that she was "the apple of her father's eye". "When he gets home, please be sure to thank him for these."

Jill left the clinic and walked back to find Enid but didn't see her anywhere. She wandered slowly up the street. No Enid. She saw a lorry parked by a wall several feet away. A loading ramp led up to its open doors. Jill wondered if Enid was hiding in it. She often jumped out of unexpected places, just to annoy Jill.

"Een!" she called through cupped hands.

"I'm here, Jill. Tuppence found a patch of dandelions." Enid appeared beside the lorry. "Come on over."

When Jill walked past the ramp, she glanced inside the lorry and something caught her eye. It was a pile of silky material – parachute material.

"Hang on, Een." Jill had to take a closer look. She climbed up into the lorry and Enid followed her.

"It's dark." Enid threw her hand across her nose. "And, phew – it smells of fuel."

"Een, come and look back here."

"What is it, Jill?" Before Jill could answer, someone slid the ramp into the lorry and clicked the rear doors shut. The cab doors opened and closed, the engine started up and the lorry lurched forward.

Jill lost her balance and fell into the pile of soft fabric, Enid tumbling on top of her.

"I can't see anything." Enid sat up, whimpering. "Quick! Bang on the wall, Jill, and get them to stop."

"No, no," whispered Jill. "They mustn't know we're here." She sat in stunned silence for a second before she spoke. "That parachute in the bushes… we're sitting on it. I think these men are spies."

Enid fell towards Jill as the lorry swung around a corner. Her eyes grew large and her voice was a hoarse whisper.

"We're being kidnapped!"

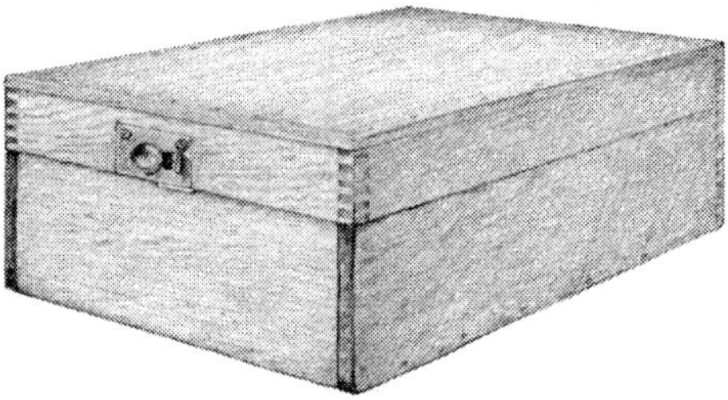

Chapter 4

Jill slid back below the cab window as the vehicle rumbled down the road. "Come and sit back here," she whispered to Een. "So the drivers won't see you."

Enid crawled towards her. In the flickering light, Jill saw how white her sister's cheeks had become.

"Are you alright, Een?"

Enid shook her head no.

"They'll… kill us." Enid whispered the words into Tuppence's shell. "We'll never see Mum and Dad again."

"Of course we will," said Jill, trying to sound certain. "The lorry will have to stop somewhere." She put her arm around Enid. "We'll escape. You'll see."

Jill tried to sound confident, like her mother had this morning when their father hadn't come home.

A cool draft blew through a crack in the floor and Jill drew her knees up close to her chest.

"Tuppence is freezing." Enid breathed on his shell in an attempt to warm him.

"Here." Jill tugged at the parachute material and wrapped a bunch of it around Tuppence. "We'll make him a nest out of some of this."

Moving the parachute dislodged a box, which fell sideways and hit the floor with a thump. Jill waited anxiously to see if the driver and his mate had heard, but the lorry kept moving along.

Jill stared at the fallen wooden box. She reached forward and grabbed the handle, but when she tried to open the case it was locked.

"Leave it alone, Jill. You'll get us into trouble."

As Jill's eyes grew accustomed to the dark she noticed a patch of oil on her skirt. Then she began to notice other things inside the lorry: a spare tire, a smaller metal box and in the corner beside her, a briefcase with leather straps and buckles.

Jill lifted the briefcase onto her lap and unfastened the leather straps. Several books and pamphlets filled the space inside. She pulled out a handful of pamphlets and held one up to catch the light.

"Hmm... this isn't in English." She squinted at the words. Some of them had dots over the vowels and she saw the word "Der". She'd seen Hitler referred to as "Der Fuhrer" in a joke in the newspaper. "It's German."

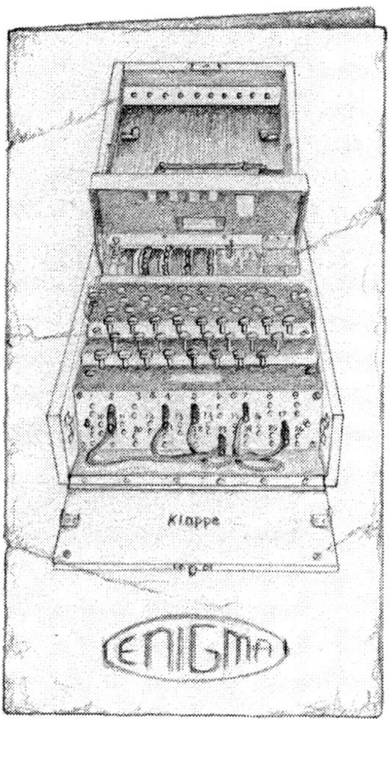

"That proves it. They're German spies." Enid nodded towards the cab. "When they find us, they'll kill us."

"We won't let them find us, Een."

Leafing through the next pamphlet, Jill saw a diagram of a typewriter with four large toothed wheels above the keys and a tangle of wires plugged into a board below them. Parts of the typewriter were labeled with additional text at the bottom of the page.

"I bet this is a diagram of what's in that box. It's some special kind of typewriter. Look at all those extra wheels and wires." Jill held the diagram out for Enid to see, but she had curled up under the parachute and refused to look.

When Jill opened another pamphlet she saw groups of letters arranged in columns. Some of the groups were all consonants and didn't look like words in any language.

"You'd like this, Een! Remember when you learned how to write secret messages at school? This is some kind of code."

Enid loved codes. She sat up and scanned the letters on the page.

"Emily White would go crazy over this," whispered Enid. "She loves codes but she's so mean I'm not telling her."

"You can't tell anyone anything until we know what this is."

A map fell out of the pamphlet. It showed a section of southeast England; Cambridge had been circled and connected in pen to a place called Bletchley.

"I've never heard of Bletchley." Jill folded the map. She took Tante Marlene's cookies out of her gas mask box and stuffed the map, the code words and the typewriter diagram into it.

"We'll have to eat these now." Jill opened the bag of cookies. "They're getting crumbly."

She nibbled on a cookie, but she wasn't very hungry. The vehicle continued along the road and Jill tried to make up a poem, but couldn't think of a word that rhymed with "misery". There was nothing to do but wait until the lorry stopped.

Jill's body began to feel stiff and sore. By now, she'd bitten off skin around both her thumbs and began working on her index finger until it bled. She pressed her thumb against it to stop the bleeding and began a mental list of do's and don'ts.

1) Don't take Een along on errands.
2) Do keep Een in sight at all times.
3) Don't walk into a stationary lorry.
4) Do get Een home safely.
5) Ditto Tuppence.

She heard traffic passing on the road and once a police siren blared. Jill hoped it was coming to rescue her and Enid but the siren faded into the distance. Enid cried a little, then lay quietly. The luminous hands on Jill's watch indicated that an hour had passed when the lorry slowed, turned a few corners, then stopped. They heard the creak of the cab doors opening and felt the vehicle wobble as the men got out.

Footsteps sounded along the side of the lorry and a voice with an accent spoke by the back door.

"I get the briefcase."

Jill barely had time to kick the briefcase towards the door before pulling Enid under the parachute beside her.

"Don't move a muscle," she whispered.

The handle cranked downwards, the door swung open and a wedge of sunlight burst into the lorry.

Jill lay perfectly still and prayed that they wouldn't be seen. One of the drivers was so close she could hear him breathing.

The briefcase with the diagrams and pamphlets stood where Jill had pushed it near the door. Jill heard it scuff along the metal floor and hoped she'd remembered to fasten the buckles.

"Shall I bring anything else?" asked the man suddenly. Jill felt him pulling on the parachute.

"This is it," she thought as Enid's nails dug deep into her arm. "They'll find us now."

"No," came the answer; the pulling stopped and the lorry doors slammed shut.

Jill knew there was no time to spare. She counted to ten and grabbed Enid's hand. Then they scooted across the metal floor, opened one of the doors and jumped.

"Run as fast as you can, Een!"

After the gloom of the lorry, the sunlight blinded them.

"I can't see," whispered Enid.

"Come on, you idiot!" Jill grabbed Enid's hand.

They raced down a grass-edged lane, turned a corner and hid behind a tall hedgerow to catch their breath. Then Jill crawled forward to look back up the lane.

The lorry was parked in front of a huge iron gate. A Home Guardsman stood on the driver's side, checking papers. He handed back the papers, saluted, then went to open the gate.

Before the vehicle moved out of view, Jill caught sight of the license plate – JTE 143.

"The lorry went through a gate," Jill whispered, crouching down beside her sister, but Enid wasn't listening.

"You called me an idiot," she whimpered, a large tear rolling down her cheek.

"I didn't mean it, Een. I was scared, too." Jill took her sister's hand. "Come on. We can't stay here."

They ran down a tree-lined lane, around another corner, and along a high wrought iron fence with barbed wire coiled along the top. Leafy thickets and trees concealed whatever lay behind the fence. A few cyclists passed by on the road beside them but Jill barely noticed. They ran until Enid tripped on the edge of a paving stone and fell heavily to the ground. Tuppence shot out of her arms and hit the pavement with a crack.

Ignoring the blood dripping from a gash in her knee, Enid crawled towards Tuppence and gently picked him up. His head and legs had disappeared inside his shell. Enid stared at him in horror.

"Look what happened!" she cried.

Jill saw that a crescent shaped piece of shell had broken off near his tail.

"It doesn't hurt him does it?"

"Of course it does. He could get an infection and die. Tortoises have nerves just like we do – even in their scutes."

"These are scutes?" asked Jill picking up the broken pieces of Tuppence's shell.

"Yes," said Enid.

"I don't suppose we could glue them back on."

"Of course not." Enid scorned the idea. "It would be like trying to glue back a fingernail."

"Well, anyway, I doubt if he'll die just yet."

Enid set Tuppence gently on her lap and rubbed his shell in slow circles. For a moment Enid seemed to have forgotten that they were miles from home. But Jill hadn't.

Where were they? Jill looked across the street at a row of red brick terraced houses, each one with a different shade of trim. Coloured glass patterns glowed in the windows, and roses, lilacs and honeysuckle grew up around the tiny patches of lawn by the front doors. It looked like Cambridge but Jill suspected it was Bletchley, the place she had seen marked on the map in the lorry. And now she had to find a way home.

"Come on Een, we have to keep moving."

"I want to see Tuppence's head."

"He'll come out when he's ready. He did after Anna scared him."

But Enid didn't want to move. "You don't care about Tuppence at all," she pouted.

Jill began to lose patience. She thought of all the times her mother had said, "Remember, you were seven once". She did remember being seven and she hadn't been nearly as bratty as Enid. Jill tried another tack.

"Look, Een, your knee's all bloody and you didn't even notice. You're very brave."

Enid brightened a little.

"Am I, really?"

"Yes, you are."

"But I don't feel brave. I want to go home." Enid looked around. "Where are we anyway?"

"I think we're in Bletchley," said Jill.

"The place on that map?" asked Enid.

"Yes."

Enid pointed at the barbed fence.

"The spies are in there, aren't they?"

"Yes." Jill squinted through the gaps in the fence. "I wish we could see who else is in there."

"I don't. They're all spies."

"I doubt it, Een. But it does look sort of secret in there. Those men in the lorry, I'm sure they're not supposed to be in there."

A large bird flew over the trees and into the compound. Enid stood up, carefully straightening her bloody knee.

"Look at that," she said tracking the bird above the trees. "It's a carrier pigeon."

"How do you know?"

"See the container strapped on its leg?" Enid pointed upwards. "That's for the messages. My book about unusual pets says that the army uses them. They can fly sixty miles and they always find their way home."

"Wow," said Jill.

"My book also said they are as smart as tortoises."

Jill was wondering just how smart that made pigeons, when she was distracted by the sound of women's voices through the fence.

"Busy morning," said one.

"Yes, I'm glad we're off," said the other.

Jill wondered what kind of work they did in a place that was of interest to spies.

"There's a game of rounders in front of the house this afternoon. Are you playing?" asked the first one.

"No. I have to get home." Their voices faded as the women walked away.

"She's going home," said Enid. "I want to go home, too."

"So do I," said Jill.

"Except for the fence, this looks a bit like our street."

"I wish it was, Een. But it isn't. Come on." Jill made

her voice sound bright and cheery the way her mother did when she gave them bad tasting medicine. She didn't know how to get home, but she couldn't say that. She had never been really lost before. There'd been that time when she was four and she'd wandered off in the toy department in Haggerty's, but she didn't know she was lost until her mother scolded her.

The road ahead sloped downhill and curved under a humpbacked bridge. Jill took Enid's hand and they began walking towards the bridge. Jill noticed first one car and then several more heading towards the bridge. A few cyclists straggled by. When Jill turned back to look, she was surprised to see more cyclists and behind them bunches of walkers. Soon she and Enid were in the middle of foot and bike traffic. Jill heard snatches of conversation.

"I've got the day off. I'm going to sleep for twenty-four hours."

"I'm seeing Freddy – whoopee!"

"See ya Monday."

Enid walked closer to Jill.

"They came from in there," she said, nodding at the fence. "They're all spies."

"They can't all be spies, Een. I think they're people who just got off work," said Jill. "I wonder where they are going."

Jill heard a whistle and saw a train lumber across the humpbacked bridge. As the engine slowed, the people around her quickened their step. “They’re heading for the station. Een!” Jill gave her sister a hug. “We can take a train back to Cambridge.”

Jill made Enid keep up as they crossed a narrow footbridge above the tracks. The train had pulled into the platform below and smoke puffed up into their faces. When they reached the platform, Jill pointed to a sign.

“See that, Een?”

“Bletchley,” read Enid. “You were right.”

A wooden board showed train schedules and Jill saw a listing for Cambridge!

“Come on, Een. We’re going home.”

Chapter 5

Jill climbed into a carriage marked "second class", pulling Enid up behind her. She walked along the train corridor, glancing into compartments to see who was already seated. The last thing she wanted was to end up sitting with someone who would ask her awkward questions. Jill picked a compartment where a young woman sat, wearing a crisp navy suit and tie. She had her nose deep in a thick book.

"Come on, Een. Let's sit here."

Enid sank into the soft leather and placed Tuppence on her lap.

"We'll be home soon," she whispered to Tuppence, gently stroking his shell to make him come out.

Other people took seats in the small compartment, lifting their luggage into racks above their heads. Soon Jill found herself squashed between Enid and the window.

When everyone was settled, the doors slammed and the guard blew his whistle. Heavy metal gears grabbed the tracks and the train lurched out of the station.

A man in a seat by the door flicked the wheel of his lighter and lit a cigarette. He blew the smoke across the aisle and it caught in Jill's throat. She turned away, trying not to cough.

"I'll open the window if you like," said the young woman opposite, putting down her book. She had a pale cream complexion and dark brown hair. When she turned towards the light, Jill saw dozens of pinpoint freckles spreading from her nose to her cheeks. Jill thought she was as pretty as Lonnie.

"Thank you," Jill said and sat back. She loved the motion of the train. It reminded her of holidays at the seaside with her parents.

"Remember when we went to Cornwall?" she whispered to Enid, who smiled.

"A little," she whispered back. "Mum and Dad were with us then."

They hadn't been to the coast since the war began. The army had mined the beaches and strung huge coils of barbed wire along the sand.

The young woman in uniform watched Enid fuss over Tuppence for a while, then she leaned forward.

"I had a tortoise when I was your age. What's her name?"

"Tuppence," said Enid in a small voice. "And it's a 'he'."

"My tortoise was a girl. Marmalade." The young woman laughed. "Can't think why I named her Marmalade. I hated the stuff until I grew older. Do you always take Tuppence when you travel?"

Enid started to answer but the conductor came by and wedged his thick frame into the compartment door.

"Tickets, please."

Jill watched passengers hand over tickets and dug in her gas mask box. She kept a few coins in it, just in case.

The conductor turned towards her and reached out his hand.

Jill gave him the coins.

"You're sixpence short, young lady."

The woman in the uniform spoke up.

"How silly of me," she said. "I have a pass and I quite forgot to get tickets for my nieces." She handed him the money. The conductor returned Jill's coins, punched out two tickets and left.

The man in the corner gave Jill a cold stare before he took another drag of his cigarette and went back to his newspaper. The young woman spoke before Jill could thank her.

"Girls, we need to stretch our legs."

Jill and Enid followed her into the corridor.

"We're not your nieces," announced Enid when the

compartment door was safely closed.

"I know you're not, but when I saw your sister hold her breath, I had to do something. My name's Claire." She reached out and shook hands.

"I'm Jill and she's Enid."

"Hello Jill, hello Enid." A few of Claire's freckles folded into the creases of her smile. "So, how come you two are traveling alone?"

Before Enid could blab out the truth, Jill intervened and in spite of her mother's lectures about setting a good example to her little sister, she didn't set one now.

"We were visiting our aunt," she lied. "And now we're going home."

Enid opened her mouth and then shut it again.

"Hmm," said Claire, considering this information. "You two are quite the travelers. When I was your age, I was a regular stick in the mud. My parents tried to send me to aunts, uncles and grandparents. No luck! I wouldn't even go to Brownie camp."

"You were a Brownie?" Enid asked, obviously taken with the notion that Claire had once been a little girl.

"Not so very long ago," said Claire laughing. "I'm not that old!"

"You must be at least as old as Lonnie."

"I suppose Lonnie's sixty-five," joked Claire, "whoever she is."

"She lives with us," said Jill. "She's twenty-two."

"Well, I'm nineteen," said Claire.

“That’s old,” said Enid.

“Een, don’t be insulting.” Nineteen seemed quite old, even to Jill, but her mother would have scolded Enid for calling Claire “old”.

“I don’t mind,” laughed Claire. “Have you been away long?”

“No,” said Jill.

“Everything’s alright?”

“Well, no.” Jill liked Claire and she was helping them. She didn’t want to lie again. Everything wasn’t alright. “Our Dad went fire fighting last night and… well.” Jill looked down at her feet. “He didn’t come home.”

“Oh,” said Claire. Her skin and even her freckles seemed to pale as she turned towards the window. When she looked back, the corners of her eyes were moist.

“Are you crying?” Enid stared at Claire as if her hair had turned green.

Claire nodded then swallowed hard. Jill saw the muscles move under the smooth skin at her throat.

“Nineteen-year-olds are allowed to cry,” she said when she spoke again.

Nobody said anything for a while and Jill stared out of the window. Farmland ribbed with newly sewn crops rolled away from the train. The track curved and the engine came into view, cutting through the fields like scissors through soft folds of green cloth.

The man who was smoking came out of the compartment and brushed so close to Jill that the buckle

of his raincoat belt caught on her gas mask. Without speaking he disentangled himself and glared at Jill before walking away down the corridor. Jill wondered why he was so unfriendly. And then she began thinking. Did he work at Bletchley Park? Could he have seen her and Enid run away from the lorry? Could he be one of the spies? "That man keeps looking at us. I think he's a spy," said Jill when he had gone. "He got on at Bletchley. Do you recognize him, Claire?"

"Loads of people work at Bletchley Park. But I've never seen him before."

"He's not wearing a uniform," said Enid.

"Not everyone wears a uniform. I do because I'm a Wren."

"That's the navy, isn't it?" said Jill.

"Yes. Wrens is a nickname for the 'Women's Royal Naval Service'. When I got out of high school, I was supposed to go to university but my mother is a nurse and my father is a fighter pilot…" Claire paused when she mentioned her father. "So I decided to do something to help in the war."

Jill was certain the war would be over before she had to find a job. She rebelled at the idea of wearing another uniform after years of her current school outfit. If she became a botanist she'd wear T-shirts and overalls out in the field.

"Do you ever go to sea?" asked Enid.

"No. Women do land jobs."

"And yours is in Bletchley?" asked Jill.

"Yes," said Claire.

"I wouldn't want to work there," said Enid. "It felt spooky with all those guards and fences."

Claire laughed.

"I like my work," she said. "And it's nice inside the park, once you get through all that barbed wire. There's grass and a lake and ducks with names. My favourite one is 'Pooh', fat like Winnie the Pooh. You'd like him, Enid."

"Did all those people who caught the train at Bletchley work where you do?" asked Jill.

"Most of them. We just changed shifts."

"What do you do in there?"

Claire hesitated.

"I help the war effort," she said.

"What do you do?" asked Enid.

"I can't say," said Claire. "Some war work is secret and the people who do it must promise not to tell."

"I know they play rounders in there," said Enid.

"How?" Claire looked at her in surprise.

"We walked by the fence and I heard someone talk about a game."

"It might have been me. We play on an old croquet lawn whenever we can." Claire grinned. "And I'm an ace batter!"

"I'm a rotten batter," said Enid. "But I'm fast at running bases."

A voice behind her made Jill turn. The man from their compartment stared down at her, and his steely blue eyes pierced hers for a second before he motioned that he wanted to pass. Feeling uneasy, Jill quickly moved aside. When the man was gone Jill whispered to Claire.

"I'm sure that man from Bletchley knows something about Een and me, and even you, Claire."

"I need to go to pee," interrupted Enid. "Please come with me, Jill."

"I'll hold Tuppence if you like," offered Claire.

Enid hesitated.

"Remember," said Claire. "I know about tortoises."

"Hold him carefully," ordered Enid. "He's getting over a bad fall and he won't come out of his shell."

"I'll whisper sweet things to him, I promise."

Enid hesitated another moment, then placed Tuppence in Claire's arms.

The train rounded another curve and Jill and Enid swayed down the corridor like sailors on a rolling sea. The sign on the toilet said "engaged" so they waited by the door and watched the ground race by through a gap between the carriages.

The sign clicked "vacant" and a woman came out. Jill and Enid crammed into the small cubicle and Enid sat down.

"It smells of pee," she said, holding her nose.

"It's because people miss the hole when the train moves," said Jill. "Hurry up, Een."

But Enid wanted to ask questions.

"Jill – why didn't you tell Claire what really happened to us?"

"We're just getting to know her."

"But she likes tortoises."

"A good thing," Jill agreed.

"Why did she cry when we told her about Dad?"

"I'm not sure. Maybe something happened to her dad. But you can't ask her."

"Why?"

"It'll make her sad again. She'll tell us if she wants to."

Enid finished up and they returned to their compartment, where Claire was waiting outside the door with Tuppence. His head was out and he was looking around.

"Tuppence!" Enid looked at Claire with new admiration. "He must really like you, Claire."

"I whispered magic words." Claire handed Tuppence back to Enid.

"What did you say?"

"If I tell I'll lose the magic."

"Everything's secret with you," Enid pouted but Claire wasn't listening.

"I've moved my bags into the next compartment, so we don't have to sit by that man from Bletchley," she said. Jill could have hugged her.

When they reached their new seats, Claire pulled

out a deck of cards.

"Let's play Old Maid."

As Claire dealt the cards, Jill studied her face and wondered why she had cried when Jill spoke of her father and how he hadn't returned from the fire. She decided that Claire's father was a fighter pilot and something must have happened to him. She remembered kissing her father before he left last night and wondered if she would ever see him again. The thought felt like a rock in her chest. She could hardly breathe as she picked up her cards and tried to concentrate on matching up the pairs.

They played three games of Old Maid. Jill won once and Enid won twice before they got tired.

"Are we there yet?" asked Enid.

"In about fifteen minutes, we'll see the suburbs of London," said Claire.

"London!" Jill jerked forward so fast she bumped Claire's elbow and all the cards fell on the floor. "Did you say London?"

"Yes," said Claire. "This is the 3:15 to London. Why?"

"We're supposed to be going to Cambridge!"

Chapter 6

Jill stared bleakly at the window and nibbled at the skin around her nails, her thoughts racing. She could see how in her rush to board she'd mistaken the London train for the one to Cambridge. Instead of getting her little sister home, they were barreling along the tracks towards London. Her father always told her to be slow and sure and pay attention to the details.

It was bad enough being on the wrong train – but the wrong train to London! She'd heard on the radio about "The Battle of Britain" and how enemy bombers had ravaged the city. Marble Arch, Trafalgar Square, Madame Tussauds and even Buckingham Palace had been hit. Who would want to go to London?

"It's alright, Jill," said Claire, as if reading her mind. "There are lots of trains from London to Cambridge.

And you know what I always say?" She leaned forward and smiled. "That something good always comes out of a mistake."

Jill couldn't think of anything good that had come of getting on the wrong train except meeting Claire, who she really liked.

"I should have read the sign carefully. Mum wouldn't have got us on the wrong train." Jill hung her head and stared blankly at an oil stain on her skirt. She refused to cry and hoped that Enid wouldn't either.

"I'll never ever see Mum and Dad again." A tear dropped from Enid's cheek onto Tuppence's shell.

"Of course you'll see your parents again, Enid." Claire spoke cheerfully. "We'll call your mother when we get to London and tell her what happened."

Jill felt glad about that but now she had a new problem. If Claire spoke to her mother she'd find out that Jill had lied about visiting an aunt in Bletchley.

"I'll talk to my mother," said Jill, quickly.

"Of course you will." Claire patted Jill's knee. "It'll all work out."

"I want Mum now," wailed Enid.

"You can talk to her when we get to London," said Claire, hugging Enid close. "Meanwhile, Jill and I will just have to do."

"Alright," said Enid, settling against Claire. Jill watched Enid pull out her handkerchief and arrange it carefully over her right hand. Then she rested the hand against her cheek and began sucking her thumb. Enid hadn't done that since she was three.

The wrong train rumbled on. Jill sat watching clumps of rose bay willow herb race by the windows like pink streamers. A crowd of crows rose squawking out of the bushes. They must be yelling at her. Even the train mocked her, beating out the words on the track.

"You-id-i-ot-you-id-i-ot-you-real-ly-are-an-id-i-ot."

Jill covered her ears until the green fields disappeared and the suburbs of London came into view. Rows of brick houses flanked the track, and lines of washing flapped like bunting in narrow backyards. Colourful shirts, pajamas and socks hung out to dry. Jill felt comforted. Normal life seemed to continue in London in spite of all the terrible stories of death and devastation she'd heard on the news. She wondered if Kew Gardens still opened its doors to visitors or if the glass in the beautiful greenhouses had been shattered by bombs.

"We're getting close." Claire smiled out the window.

"Do you live in London?" asked Enid.

"Yes, when I'm not in Bletchley," said Claire. "I'm going home to see my mother."

"Are there lots of air raids in London?" asked Enid.

"There have been," said Claire. "But Londoners go about their business just like people everywhere else. Children go to school, mums go shopping and people go to work."

They left the houses behind and brick factories appeared on either side of the train tracks, their walls advertising cigarettes, food products, movies and most of all, war slogans.

"Dig for Victory, Plant a Victory Garden!" A farmer holding baskets laden with vegetables smiled out of the poster, a pitchfork across his shoulder. Jill had read that Londoners planted vegetables in Hyde Park and even kept pigs.

"Less Light, Less Speed" said another poster featuring a car, with shaded headlights, driving down a pitch-black street.

"Join the Wrens and Free a Man for the Fleet!"

"That's you, Claire," said Enid as they passed the sign. Enid put away her handkerchief and sat up. "I want to be a Wren when I'm old enough."

"I hope the war will be over when you're old enough." Claire smiled.

The train slowed and the tracks multiplied, separating the buildings like giant metal zippers.

"King's Cross," called out the conductor.

Wheels screeched against brake metal. The train pulled under a high glass canopy and came to a stop. "You won't like it here, Tuppence," Enid whispered to Tuppence's shell. "It's loud and busy."

"He'll be fine Enid and so will you. Come on girls." Claire hoisted her bags off the luggage rack. "Let's find a phone and call your mother."

The engine released a final blast of steam. The door swung open and Jill stepped down onto the platform. She gripped Enid's hand, making sure they stayed close to Claire. High stone arches flanked King's Cross station, rising up to support the glass canopy above their heads. Jill turned back once and saw the man from Bletchley looking at her through the crowd. She tightened her grip on Enid.

The station seemed busier than when Jill's class had come to London to see the Egyptian "Mummies" at the British Museum before the war began. A large board announced arrivals and departures and people stared up at it, checking their watches. A porter guided a suitcase-laden cart around two soldiers kissing their girlfriends goodbye.

"Why are all those people wearing those blue and yellow scarves?" Enid pointed at a noisy group coming in from the street.

"They're football fans. There's a game at Wembley Stadium," said Claire. "But more importantly – here's a phone booth."

Tucked behind a pillar, Jill saw the corner of a red telephone booth. She'd have to tell Claire the truth about how they got to Bletchley, but before she could, Claire dialed the operator and handed her the phone.

"Give the operator your number," said Claire.

Jill took the phone. The line connected and she

waited for ten rings, while Enid jumped up and down chanting "Mum, Mum, Mum". No one answered. Why wasn't her mother at home? She always sat down on Saturday afternoons and darned socks while she listened to "The Robinsons" on the radio. "Time to put my feet up," she would say and Lonnie would make some tea.

"She's not there." Jill hung up. Enid stopped jumping and crumpled into a heap on the station floor. She hid her face in her hands.

"I want Mum," she sobbed.

"We'll try later, dear. She'll be home then." Claire put her arm around Enid's shoulder. "I bet you're starving. Let's go to the café and grab a bite to eat."

They walked past a sign for the underground train. Jill had ridden the tube, as Londoners called it, a few times. A notice said "Shelter opens at 4:30 p.m.".

"Do people shelter down there?" asked Jill.

"Yes," said Claire. "They sleep on the platforms."

"But why don't they use Morrison shelters like we do?"

"Many do, but some people feel safer sleeping underground. Look," said Claire. "There's a café."

The station café offered few choices – baked beans on toast, sticky buns, tea, milk, cucumber or spam sandwiches. Jill thought spam was disgusting, even though her mother said it was clever of the Americans to invent it. She chose cucumber sandwiches and slid her tray along the counter towards the cashier. Jill reached for the coins in her gas mask box but Claire opened her bag and pulled out her purse. "Keep your money, Jill. You may need it."

"Mum will pay you back." Jill knew her mother would have wanted her to pay. Reluctantly she put her money away.

Claire carried the tray to the table but when she set it down, the clasp of her bag caught on the chair and the bag fell open. Jill ducked under the table to gather up the contents.

"Thanks," said Claire. Jill handed her a lipstick, a handkerchief, some keys and a small cloth sack containing something heavy. The way Claire snatched the little sack made Jill wonder what it was, but she knew it would be rude to ask. From under her chair, Enid retrieved a small mirror and a dog-eared photo of a man and woman.

"Is that your Mum and Dad, Claire?" asked Enid.

"Yes." Claire smiled at the photograph.

"Your Dad's in an Air Force uniform."

"Yes. The picture was taken just after the war began."

"Will you see your Dad while you're in London?"

Claire ran her finger over her father's face.

"I'd love to see him. But I can't. He's a prisoner of war in Germany."

"I'm sorry," said Enid before Jill could scold her. "I suppose I shouldn't have asked."

Claire put the photo back in her bag.

"It's not your fault, Enid," she said. "It's this stupid war. And anyway, you told me about your father, so why shouldn't you know about mine?"

"Actually," said Jill, "I didn't tell you the whole story. And if you like, I'll tell you now."

"I'm ready," Claire pulled her chair in close.

"It all started when I saw a plane above the woods near our house." Jill told Claire about walking through the woods that morning and finding the parachute. When she got to the part about getting into the lorry Jill said, "That was my first mistake. My second mistake was lying to you about visiting an aunt."

"It did seem odd that she put you on a wrong train," admitted Claire.

"When we escaped from the lorry, I looked back and saw the registration number – JTE 143."

"Good thinking, Jill." Claire wrote the number on her paper napkin and put it in her purse.

When Jill described the pamphlets she'd taken from the briefcase, Claire pulled her chair even closer.

"The letters looked like codes," said Enid.

"I need those pamphlets." Claire's voice was urgent. "I know what they are and I'll make sure they go where they belong." Claire glanced around the café. The only other customers sat near the door. "You've got to trust me," she whispered.

The decision was easy. Jill handed over the pamphlets. Claire had just put them in her bag when a voice said, "What a surprise!"

Charles stood at their table, his hands stuffed into his pockets and a wedge of papers stuffed under one arm.

"Hello Jill! Enid! Claire! This looks like a party."

"Charles!" said Enid. "What are you doing here?"

"I could ask the same of you," said Charles. He reached for a chair, spilling papers around him.

"Charles lives in our house," Enid said to Claire. "And Claire rescued us," she explained to Charles.

"From the enemy?" said Charles. He gathered up his papers and sat down.

"Sort of," said Jill, before Enid could say more. "But we should let Claire tell the story, Een."

"It's all right, Jill." Claire leaned back in her chair and stretched out her legs. "Charles knows about my work."

"How could he?" said Enid. "He teaches maths in Cambridge."

"I get around," said Charles mysteriously. "And sometimes I'm needed in London."

"In London?" asked Jill.

"Yes. I got a phone call at lunch time and I came right down."

Enid told him all about the spies and the lorry taking them to Bletchley and how they'd run away without the spies even seeing them. Charles sat forward in his chair listening, his hands fidgeting with things in his jacket pockets. Like Claire, he seemed particularly concerned

about the contents of the lorry, and especially the pamphlets.

"You deserve a medal, Jill," he said and turned to Claire. "May I help in any way? I could take the pamphlets to the office."

"Don't worry Charles," said Claire. "I'll do it."

Jill felt relieved. However much she adored Charles, Jill knew he had a habit of losing things.

Charles stood up, bumping the table with his knee, and Claire's tea slopped into her saucer. He looked at Jill and Enid.

"I wish I could take you home, but the work I have to do will last through the afternoon."

"That's all right," said Jill.

"If you're with Claire I know you'll be fine," said Charles. "London is a big confusing place."

"And today," said Claire, "all the football fans have come to watch the game at Wembley."

"Well, I'll be going then," said Charles.

As he left the café, he turned to wave and bumped into a woman coming in. Jill tried not to giggle.

It felt strange seeing Charles in King's Cross station. Jill hadn't known he did special work for the government in London. She wondered what other special things he did.

"I don't suppose you'll tell me what Charles has to do with your work in Bletchley," said Jill.

"No, I can't." Claire smiled. "Isn't it a coincidence, us both knowing him?"

"I'm glad you're in charge of those secret pamphlets, Claire," said Jill. "Charles is always losing things. Mum says he's absent-minded and Dad told me he once saw Charles cycle down the street in his slippers. I'd be mortified if I wore my slippers to school. Charles doesn't seem to care about stuff like that."

Claire looked at her watch. "Come on. It's time to try your mother again."

This time Mum answered.

"Mum, it's me, Jill. We're fine but we're in London." Jill explained what had happened, then put Enid on.

"I miss you, Mum. I want to come home." Enid all but dissolved into tears when she heard their mother's voice. "Yes, I'm being careful. I… I…" she gulped, clutching the phone like a life line. Gently Claire pried her fingers loose and took the phone.

"I'm Claire," she said. "Please don't worry. The girls are safe and I can put them on the next train to Cambridge." Claire paused and listened. "That'll work too," she said and handed the phone to Jill. "Your mother has a different plan."

When Jill finished talking she told Enid the new plan.

"Mum doesn't want us traveling alone so Tante Marlene and Fritz offered to drive to London and pick us up."

"Goody." Enid clapped her hands.

"We're to meet them on the bench outside the café," said Jill. Claire had promised Mum she'd wait until Fritz and Tante Marlene arrived.

"Who are Fritz and Tante Marlene?" asked Claire. "Those sound like German names."

"Remember when Een said you looked as old as Lonnie," said Jill. "Well, Fritz is Lonnie's husband. They're German refugees and live at our house. Tante Marlene is Fritz's sister. She's married to an English doctor."

"Yesterday Fritz helped me fix a maze for Tuppence and he knew just how to do it," said Enid.

Claire got quiet and began pushing crumbs around on her plate. Jill knew she was thinking about her father being held by Nazis in Germany.

"Fritz and Tante Marlene aren't Nazis, you know."

"Well, even so," Claire's voice was bitter. "They're still Germans. I'm sorry, but I can't imagine having Germans as friends."

Jill was surprised. She hadn't expected this reaction from Claire. She felt bad for Fritz and Marlene. They hated the Nazis and they helped with the war effort just like everybody else in England.

"I'll have to believe that they're O.K." said Claire, making an effort to smile. "Come on then. We need to get these pamphlets to my office and be back here in time to meet your friends."

Claire led Jill and Enid towards the escalator. "How would you like to ride on the tube?"

"Tuppence won't like it," said Enid. "It's dark down there."

"I thought Tuppence liked dark places," said Jill.

"He likes small cozy holes – not huge tunnels."

They bought their tickets and stepped onto the escalator, which took them down long burrowing tunnels to the train platforms. The air grew warm and stale. An array of posters passed on the tiled walls and Enid read as many as she could out loud.

"Vera Lynn at the Palladium – *Lend a Hand on the Land* – George Formby in *Spare a Copper* at the Gaumont – *Look Out in the Blackout* – Clark Gable in *Boom Town.*" Enid glanced mischievously at her sister. "Jill has a crush on Clark Gable."

Clark Gable smiled out at Jill from the poster, his beautiful white teeth flashing beneath a trimmed moustache. Jill turned pink. She was glad Charles had left. Enid might decide to say that Jill had a crush on Charles too – but she didn't.

"I think Clark is absolutely gorgeous." Claire faked a swoon. "Jill has good taste."

They walked through the tunnels and heard a train rumble in the distance."Come on," said Claire.

They reached the platform at the same time as the train. It stopped, the doors slid open and they stepped inside.

"You sit with Tuppence," said Claire, gently pushing Enid into an empty seat.

As the train moved out of the station, six "King's Cross" signs passed the windows with increasing speed. Then they were in a black tunnel. Claire reached up and grabbed a strap above Jill's head. Jill held onto a post by the doors and stared at her reflection in the glass. Her face frowned back at her. If her mother had been here, Jill knew she would have said, "Smile dear – you look too serious". Jill didn't feel like smiling.

She looked down. Enid was whispering something into Tuppence's shell. Jill felt glad Enid had him to worry about. When Tuppence's nose emerged, Enid smiled.

Jill turned back to the window. She watched people's reflections sway alongside her until her eyes settled into a hypnotic stare. She was beginning to feel sleepy when she noticed a familiar face in the glass. The man from Bletchley was staring right at her. The back of her neck felt hot. She had forgotten all about him.

When they got off the train at Victoria they wove through more passages to the Northern Line. As they boarded the second train, Jill saw the man from Bletchley dash onto the platform and jump into the rear carriage before the doors closed.

"Claire," Jill whispered. "We're being followed."

Chapter 7

Jill grabbed a handhold to steady herself then watched the man from Bletchley push his way through the passengers in the next carriage. He worked his way towards the connecting doors. Jill's knees felt weak. She touched Claire's arm.

"Look, Claire, that man from Bletchley is in the next carriage."

What did that man want from her? Maybe he didn't want her at all. Maybe it was Claire he was after. Had he been spying on them in the café and seen Claire put the pamphlets in her bag?

Claire tightened her grip on her bag. The train pulled into St. James's Park station. When the doors opened Jill wanted to run.

"Stay close," said Claire. "And don't look back."

They moved with the crowd along the platform and up out of the ground, blinking like badgers in the daylight.

At the ticket barrier, Claire couldn't find the tickets. She dug around in her handbag while impatient passengers piled up behind her.

"Step on it, lady," said a man pushing from behind.

"Ah, here they are," Jill heard Claire say before the crowd propelled her and Enid towards the street. When Jill turned to ask which way next, she couldn't see Claire. She skimmed the crowd, looking for Claire's Wren hat.

"Where's Claire?" asked Enid.

"She's coming," said Jill. But Claire didn't come.

Perhaps she had overtaken them. Jill looked up the street. She couldn't remember ever seeing this many people in London, and wondered if it was because of the football final. Traffic filled the road and a woman stepped out to wave down a taxicab. A dog raised its leg and peed on a wall of sandbags piled like plump pillows against the buildings. The air smelled dusty and dirty. A man selling newspapers waved one in the air shouting, "Cup final results! Liverpool burns! Read all about it!"

Liverpool! Families shipped their children from Liverpool to safety in Canada and Jill had read how badly the city had already been bombed. She shivered. London must be due for another attack.

"Where's Claire?" asked Enid again.

"I don't know," said Jill.

What had happened to her? Jill knew she wouldn't leave them. Had she been detained by a friend? Or an enemy? Possibilities crowded into Jill's head as she gazed at the busy street. People hurried by, paying no attention to her and Enid. A wave of fear spread from her chest to her knees.

"Claire wouldn't leave us," said Enid. "Spies took her! That's what's happened! And they'll take us next and we'll never get home and I'm scared." Enid stopped for breath. "I want Mum!" She covered her face with her arms, leaned into the wall and sobbed.

For a moment Jill felt herself panic. She couldn't take any more of Enid's blubbering. She didn't want to be in charge. She also wanted to see her mother and hear her father say everything was all right. But she knew she had to keep herself and Enid going. Without the name of Claire's London office, they couldn't go further. Only one choice remained.

"Come on, Een." She put her arm around Enid and wiped the smudges off her little sister's face. "We have to get Tuppence home. We're going back to King's Cross Station. That's where Fritz and Tante Marlene are meeting us and I have enough money for the tube."

Enid's hand felt very small as it slipped into Jill's. When they got back to King's Cross they took the escalator up, found a bench outside the café and waited for Fritz and Tante Marlene.

When Enid had settled down with Tuppence on her

lap, there was nothing else to do but look around. She thought the station very grand with its massive stone pillars and steel arches curving up to support a high glass canopy. Before her, a wide open space accommodated the comings and goings of travelers, some stopping to check a large board for train times. Beyond the space, tracks and platforms ran from under the canopy into a patch of blue sky beyond.

Jill scanned the crowd before her. When she saw a Wren hat, she jumped up, but it wasn't Claire. All around her families welcomed home their men in uniform – husbands, sons and fathers. Jill imagined her father walking out of the crowd to take her and Enid home. She wondered if Fritz and Tante Marlene were getting close to London.

"Jill," said Enid after a while.

"What?"

"Tuppence needs to pee," she said.

Jill didn't want to move. She could never fathom how Enid determined Tuppence's needs and how she acted like Tuppence could talk.

"We need to stay here," said Jill irritably. "We might miss Fritz and Tante Marlene."

"But he has to go," insisted Enid.

"Oh all right." Jill led Enid and Tuppence through one of the stone arches to the curb outside. "But he'd better be quick."

The setting sun glinted off a fleet of huge elongated

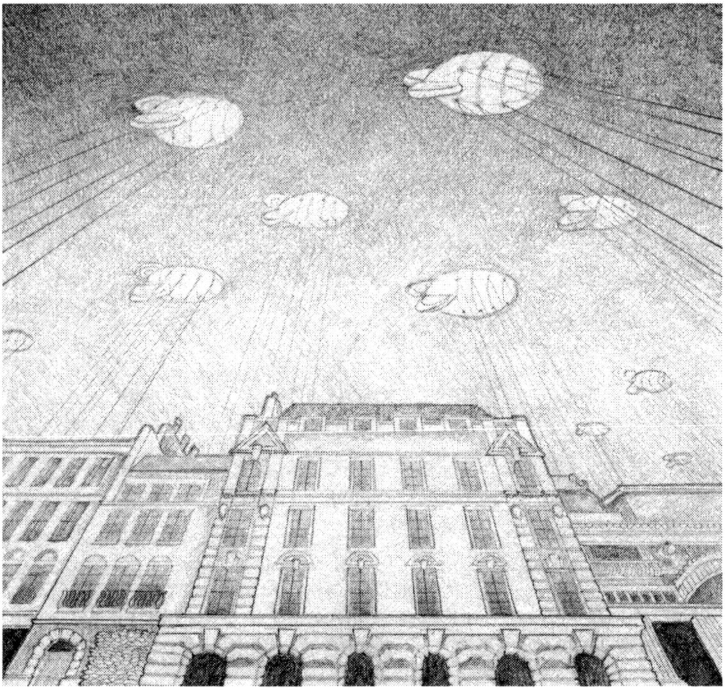

silver balloons used to prevent German bomber planes from flying low.

"Wow," said Jill. "I've never seen so many barrage balloons."

Enid squinted into the sun. "Ooh Jill. Does this mean we're going to be bombed?"

"Not necessarily. I think the balloons are just in case."

"I hope the German planes fly into them and crash," said Enid, setting Tuppence down on a patch of grass.

"Hurry up, Hattie," said a woman to a small carrot-haired girl in a green dress.

The woman dragged a pile of bedding behind her in a small cart. She reached her free hand towards the little girl.

"You have to keep up."

"No. Not coming," said Hattie slowing to a standstill, her lower lip pushed forward and her arms clasped defiantly across her chest.

A boy about Jill's age followed them, carrying a suitcase. He was twice as tall as Hattie and dressed in grey flannel shorts and a school blazer.

"Move, Hattie," he said patiently.

"Wanna sleep in my bed!" Hattie threw her teddy bear on to the sidewalk and stamped her foot. The bear landed on the grass near Tuppence.

"I'm running out of patience, Hattie," said the woman. She was tall and slim with full lips and Hattie's carrot hair. Even though she sounded tired, her voice was soft and her eyes kind.

"Get her teddy bear, Lewis, please."

The boy bent to pick it up but Enid reached it first. She smiled at Lewis and returned the bear to Hattie.

"Say thank you, Hattie," said her mother.

Hattie stood speechless. She had noticed Tuppence at Enid's feet and pointed a chubby finger.

"She likes your tortoise," said Lewis.

Enid smiled at Lewis again and he grinned back.

This time, Jill smiled too but Lewis didn't notice. It irked Jill how easily Enid got along with boys. Enid said it was because they were interested in bugs and reptiles, just like she was.

"Tortuss," said Hattie, her hand still pointing at Tuppence.

"Come on, Hattie. Mummy's leaving. If you come quickly, I'll tell you the story about the tortoise and the hare when we get settled."

Hattie agreed to this and she and Lewis followed their mother into the station.

Other families passed by, hauling bedding and suitcases.

"What are they doing?" asked Enid.

"They're going to sleep in the underground station, like Claire said."

Two men stopped and looked up at the clear blue sky.

"It's a bomber's night tonight – eh?" said one.

Enid snatched up Tuppence.

"They're talking about bombs." She pulled Jill towards the station. "Let's go down to the underground platforms."

"No. We can't," said Jill. "We said we'd wait by the café for Fritz and Tante Marlene."

"If Mum was here, she'd want us to go down." Enid kept pulling.

Jill knew her mother would want them to be safe but she would also want them to meet Fritz and Tante Marlene.

"I'm deciding and we're staying up here," said Jill, her voice rising. "You're taking care of Tuppence."

"Well, Tuppence knows it's safer underground." Enid was shouting now.

"Stop yelling, stupid, everyone's looking at us." Jill held her sister's arm and tried to clamp a hand on her mouth but Enid broke free and holding Tuppence with both hands, she ran back into the station.

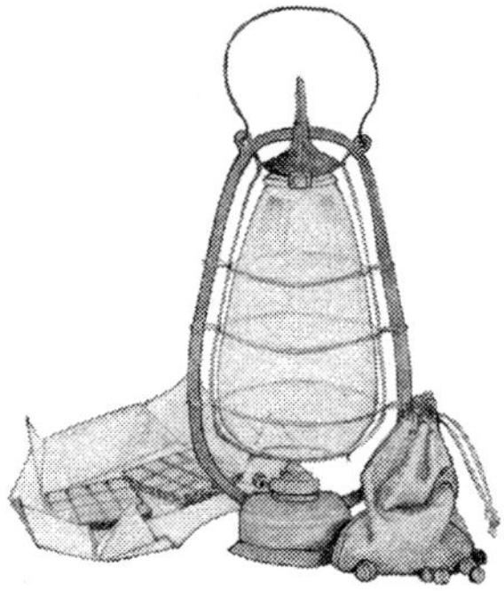

Chapter 8

Jill sprinted after her, grabbed Enid's arm and spun her round. "Don't you ever run away from me again." Jill gripped her sister's shoulders, pulling her nose to nose. "Do you understand? What if I lost you? What would Mum say then? How can you be such an idiot?" Jill fired out the questions like flack from an enemy plane. She glared angrily at her sister.

Speechless for once, Enid folded meekly into Jill's chest and sobbed. Jill took her hand and led her back to the bench outside the café. They sat quietly until Enid's sobs became sniffs and occasional hiccups.

"Jill," said Enid between sniffs. "I'm frightened. Make up a poem about Tuppence, something special about him. Please."

Jill didn't feel like making up a poem about a stupid tortoise but she wasn't angry any more.

"Please," repeated Enid.

Tortoise words began to gather inside Jill's head.

"O.K., Een. Here's your poem:

'If a turtle wants to swim he will,
But Tuppence is terrestrial.
He makes his bed
Inside the shed
And dreams of things celestial.'"

"What are 'things celestial'?" asked Enid.

"Heavenly things."

"That's good, Jill. Tuppence," Enid gently stroked his shell, "I hope you're having celestial dreams."

Enid made Jill repeat the poem enough times so that she could memorize it and then she lay down with her head across Jill's knees and fell asleep, saying, "I'll dream of things celestial."

When the station clock struck 8:00, they were still waiting. Jill's stomach gurgled and she had pins and needles in her legs but she didn't want to disturb Enid.

Hattie's mother came by on her way to the toilet.

"I'm Mrs. Parsons," she said. "Are you girls alone?"

"We're waiting for some friends." Jill didn't say their names, fearing Mrs. Parsons might react to Fritz and Tante Marlene being German.

"When are they coming?"

"Soon, I hope," said Jill.

Enid awoke shivering and sat up.

"Why don't you come and join us down on the platform until your friends get here," said Mrs. Parsons. "We've plenty of blankets and you'll be comfortable. Just write a note and leave it on the bench. We can come back up and check in a while." Mrs. Parsons pulled a pencil and some paper out of her handbag.

Enid was wide awake now and Jill could tell how badly she wanted to go down, but this time she didn't beg.

Jill gave in. She wrote a note and stuck it on the bench with an old band-aid she found in her pocket. They followed Mrs. Parsons down the escalator onto the platform.

"Wow," said Jill when she saw the platform. Hundreds of people were wedged side by side along the wall with blankets and pillows everywhere.

A train came out of the tunnel. Passengers got off and on and a guard said, "Mind the gap," as the doors closed.

Mrs. Parsons led Jill and Enid past a group of teenagers. The boys were playing cards and the girls sat behind them, whispering and giggling at each other. An elderly man with knobby finger joints lay beside his wife on the concrete. A glass of water containing a set of false teeth stood by his pillow.

"Ooh, Elsie," said the old man shifting heavily onto his side. "This sack of bones may never get up again."

Elsie, her hair in a net over tightly pinned curls, leaned over and straightened his covers.

"Mind you don't spill your teeth, dear," she said, giving him a peck on the cheek.

"Een, don't stare," said Jill, dragging her sister by the old couple.

They reached the spot where Lewis sat with Hattie on his lap. His long arms held her chubby waist as she leaned forward to grab at his knee socks.

"There!" she said with satisfaction, as she pushed first one and then the other down around his ankles. Lewis looked grumpy, but when he saw Jill and Enid he managed a smile. Dimples formed in his cheeks like Clark Gable's, Jill thought.

Hattie broke loose and ran towards her mother. Lewis pulled up his socks and laid out two extra blankets for Jill and Enid.

"Here, Lewis," said Mrs. Parsons handing Lewis some money. "I'm sure we're all starving. Please get us some sandwiches and tea."

Lewis took the money and walked along the platform to the Women's Auxiliary Service canteen at the far end.

Mrs. Parsons settled herself against the wall with Hattie in her lap.

"Do make yourselves comfortable, girls," she said, patting the blankets beside her. "It's hardly home, but it's the best we can do."

Lewis came back holding a large tray and passed out jam sandwiches and cups of hot tea. Then he sat down between Jill and Enid.

Jill was hungry and took large bites of bread and jam as she listened to the people around her. A mother yelled at her son for standing too close to the edge of the platform. A few blankets away, two young men strumming banjos sang a George Formby song. They had changed the words from "sitting on the corner of the street to watch a certain little lady go by" to "sitting on the dirty station platform waiting for the Gerries to drop a bomb". When a second train entered the station a baby woke and cried. Jill couldn't imagine getting any rest in a place like this.

"You'd need to be a cryptodiran to sleep in this racket," Enid said to Lewis.

Jill rolled her eyes.

"Yes," he said. "Mum puts cotton in her ears. But I'd much rather be tucked up inside a shell."

For once, Jill wished she knew more about tortoises.

"Do you like tortoises, Lewis?" Enid asked.

"I'm an avid herpetologist." Lewis pulled a book on reptiles out of his school bag and passed it to Enid. But instead of talking about snakes with Enid, Lewis turned to Jill.

"I gather you're not interested in cold-blooded creatures." Lewis grinned and the dimples returned.

"No," said Jill. "I prefer botany."

"Oh," said Lewis flatly. Botany must sound incredibly boring to him. Jill decided to change the subject.

"Do the trains run all night?"

"No. They stop at 10:30," said Lewis. "We've sheltered down here a lot. I know the routine."

Mrs. Parsons opened her suitcase and took out a Grey Rabbit book.

"Little Grey Rabbit and the Weasels," she began.

Hattie popped her thumb back in her mouth and nestled into her mother's side.

"I have that book." Enid leaned closer to listen.

"It's a good story," said Mrs. Parsons, slipping an arm around Enid's shoulders.

While Enid and Hattie listened to the story, Jill sat back against the cold tiles and thought about the day. What had happened to Claire? Had Charles managed to get back to Cambridge? Then she let herself think about her father. It seemed like ages since she'd seen him. So much had happened since she got up this morning that she'd hardly had time to think. Now the possibilities crowded in. A wall had collapsed on him. He'd inhaled smoke and passed out. He'd fallen off a ladder and broken bones. Jill bit the loose flaps of skin around her thumb. She could feel Lewis watching her with his kind grey eyes. She wanted to tell him how worried she was but instead she said, "Where's your dad?"

"He's in the navy," said Lewis. "I haven't seen him for a month."

"Oh," said Jill.

"He writes whenever he can but he's not allowed to say where he is."

"Because the Nazis might get hold of the letters?"

"Yes, that's right. What about your dad?"

"He's…" Jill was determined not to cry. "I'm not sure…"

"You don't have to say." Lewis jumped up and

reached out a hand. "Come on. I'll show you what I do when I get bored down here."

Mrs. Parsons looked up.

"Stay away from the platform edge you two and I want you both back in half an hour," she said.

Lewis pulled up his socks, which were loose now that Hattie had stretched them out. His bare knees showed below the hem of his grey flannel shorts. He took Jill's hand and she followed him along the platform. Jill never held hands with boys in Cambridge. Her friends would tease each other about things like that, but here in London, a hundred feet under the ground with bombs about to fall, it felt fine. Lewis seemed shy and confident at the same time. He must have all kinds of responsibilities while his father was away fighting.

"There's a chocolate machine over there," he said. "I'm eating as much chocolate as I can before it goes on rationing."

Jill's family hardly ever bought chocolate and she watched with delight as Lewis pushed some pennies into the slot and pulled out a blue-wrapped Cadbury bar. He gave Jill half.

With chocolate melting in their mouths, they walked past a group of children playing hopscotch near the escalators. The chocolate seemed to energize Lewis.

"Beat you to the top," he said, running up a down escalator as fast as he could. Her mother's disapproving face flashed through Jill's mind, but she couldn't resist.

They raced each other up then let the moving stairs carry them down backwards.

When Jill needed to pee, Lewis found the toilets and when she was thirsty he found her water. Every now and then he threw her a quick smile. Jill felt comfortable around him, so she told him about the two people from Cambridge who were coming to get her.

"They're Germans," said Jill.

"Refugees," said Lewis. "I'll bet you get teased a lot for being friends with them."

"How'd you guess?"

"Nobody I know likes Germans."

"Do you mind them?" asked Jill.

"I feel bad for the refugees. It can't be any fun being chased out of your homeland. I never want to leave London." Lewis looked at his watch.

"Do we have to go back yet?" Jill wished that Lewis lived in Cambridge, not London.

"We still have eight minutes. Come on."

A train had pulled onto the platform and before the doors were closed, Lewis grabbed Jill's hand and pulled her inside.

"Wow, Lewis," Jill giggled. "Won't your Mum be mad at us?"

"She won't know. I do it all the time. It's better than just sitting around on the platform waiting for the bombs to fall."

"Do you ever get lost?"

"No. I ride for a few stations, then get off and go back."

The train clattered through the tunnel.

"Euston," Jill read at the next station.

As the doors opened, Jill heard a dull thud above. A few people whispered "air raid" but everyone stayed calm until the train lights went out and the doors stuck half open. Then people screamed and pushed forward. Jill and Lewis were near the door and were able to squeeze out through the narrow gap. The smell of burning metal filtered through the air as they waited for a train back to King's Cross. Lewis seemed calm but Jill was terrified. What would they do if they couldn't get back?

Another train came and Jill marveled at how the trains kept running in spite of a raid.

"Thank goodness you're safe," said Mrs. Parsons when she saw them. "There was a strike down the lines. Didn't you hear the siren?"

"Yes," said Lewis. "Sorry we're late."

"Before the strike, Enid, Hattie and I went upstairs to see if your friends had arrived, but they hadn't," added Mrs. Parsons.

A pang of guilt shot through Jill.

"Thank you, Mrs. Parsons. I can't believe I forgot about that."

"It's all right dear. You've had a long day."

"They should have been here by now," said Jill with growing concern.

"The raid may have delayed them," said Mrs. Parsons.

"I'm not going anywhere in London tonight," Enid announced. "I'm staying down here."

"That's a good idea," said Mrs. Parsons. "It's the safest place."

Lewis leaned over and whispered into Jill's ear. "Mom would say we're safe even if the roof was falling in."

Jill smiled. She thought about how her own mother acted like things were normal even though nothing about a war was normal. If they had to stay, Jill didn't mind spending a little extra time with Lewis. She prepared herself for a night underground. The platform wasn't as cramped as the Morrison shelter back home but the air smelled of fuel and cigarette smoke. Jill scratched at some bug bites on her arms.

"Mosquitoes," said Lewis. "They like these warm damp tunnels."

"Tuppence eats mosquitoes," said Enid.

"He's welcome," said Lewis.

Enid crawled around looking for mosquitoes.

"Don't get near the track, Een," said Jill. Then she whispered to Lewis, "Do people ever roll onto the track in their sleep and get electrocuted?"

"They turn the electricity off when the trains stop running at 10:30."

The air raid brought more people below ground. By

10:30 the platform became so crowded that people began to climb onto the tracks and sit between the rails.

A voice called out, "Let's have a song!" and "There Will Always be an England" filled the air.

Half an hour later, the lights shook as several explosions sounded somewhere above them. Enid hid under a blanket. With each blast above ground Hattie's wails joined those of other frightened children on the platform.

"Mummy's here, dear." Mrs. Parsons tried to cover her ears, but Hattie pushed her away.

Jill stared at the platform ceiling, hoping it wouldn't cave in. She wondered what was happening to Tante Marlene and Fritz and Claire and Charles above ground.

The Salvation Army band tuned their instruments and began playing hymns. It felt like a funeral.

"And did those feet, in ancient times, walk upon England's mountains green…" sang a few voices. Jill perked up.

"Een, we sing this at school."

Jill sang but her voice sounded small and frightened.

"Maybe school will be closed on Monday," joked Lewis but Jill didn't feel like laughing. She wanted this day to be a bad dream. She wanted to wake up beside her mother and father at home in Cambridge. She covered her mouth with her hand so Lewis wouldn't see her lips trembling.

"Let's play marbles." Lewis pulled a small bag out of his pocket.

"They'll roll away," said Jill dully.

"We'll make a barricade."

Jill watched Lewis divide his marbles.

"You can keep the ones you win," he said. Jill held a marble to the light and admired the swirls in the glass balls.

"Are you sure? These are beautiful marbles."

"I know." He grinned. "I plan to win them all back."

Lewis drew a circle with a piece of chalk and released his marbles inside it. They glinted in the dim light.

"You go first," said Lewis.

Jill scoped out her best shots, chose a greenish blue marble near the edge of the circle and aimed her marble at it. "Clink" – it hit and the marbles rolled out against the barricade.

"There's one I won't get back," said Lewis, handing the blue green one to Jill.

They played until another explosion rattled the platform and the lights went out. An air raid warden appeared and the crowd stilled.

"It's bad," he said. "The Gerries are out to get us tonight."

Jill reached for Enid and held her close in the dark.

"Want my bed," cried Hattie, her voice rising above the singers.

"You're fine, Hattie," Mrs. Parsons said. Jill didn't feel fine at all and Hattie continued to cry.

Hurricane lanterns were lit and cast long, black shadows on the tunnel walls.

"Monster shadows," said Lewis. His hands shaped a Tyrannosaurus head in front of one of the lanterns and he danced it across the wall.

Jill didn't understand how Lewis could play with shadows while the bombs fell above.

"I'd hate living in London," she said, "and spending nights down here in this awful place. How can you stand it, Lewis?"

"It's where I live," said Lewis simply. "I love London."

"But aren't you scared?" whispered Jill.

"Of course I am. But I wouldn't want Mum or Hattie to know." Lewis pulled a flashlight out of his bag and flipped it on. The beam sliced through the shadows and pooled between the tracks like yellow water. Then it slid up to the vaulted ceiling, searching out cracks in the tunnel. A broken pipe hung from one.

"At least it's not a water pipe," said Lewis. Water pipes would mean flooding and Jill didn't want to think about the consequences. She could barely think at all. Her head felt heavy. She lay down on a blanket beside Enid. The last thing she heard before she fell asleep was a group singing "The London I Love".

Chapter 9

Jill dreamt she was lying on the cool dirt at home in her garden. Suddenly, the ground fell away beneath her and she landed in the cellar under the college clinic. All the files had fallen off the shelves and she was crawling through them, looking for her father, when a voice called from above.

"Wake up, Jill. Wake up."

The smell of lavender drifted above her and when she looked up, a large bosom came into focus, hovering above her like a barrage balloon.

"We are late, my darling, Fritz and I. But at last we are here!" Tante Marlene leaned towards Jill, the tip of her cigarette glowing in the half light.

"What time is it?" asked Jill as Tante Marlene planted a wet kiss on her cheek. Her throat felt like sandpaper and her neck was stiff, but it didn't matter. Tante Marlene and Fritz were here.

Fritz bent over Enid and shook her awake. "Open your eyes, Meine Kleine."

Blinking sleepily, Enid sat up and reached under the covers for Tuppence. "Can we go home now?" she said, a smile spreading across her face.

"Yes," said Fritz.

Now that Tante Marlene and Fritz were there the dreary platform seemed almost cheerful. Jill forgot how hopeless she'd felt the night before. They were going home.

"Mrs. Parsons," Jill whispered, gently nudging her awake. Mrs. Parsons sat up, frowning and adjusting her clothes.

"Good morning," said Tante Marlene brightly, reaching a hand towards Mrs. Parsons. "It must be very uncomfortable sleeping on the concrete."

"It's fine if you're used to it," Mrs. Parsons said coldly. "And who are you?" She stood without taking Tante Marlene's hand.

"I am Marlene." Tante Marlene smiled politely. "You must be Claire."

"No. I'm Pam Parsons."

Enid dragged Fritz forward. "This is Fritz, Mrs. Parsons," she said. "He's Lonnie's husband and Anna's daddy and he's an air raid warden in Cambridge."

Mrs. Parsons wouldn't look at either Fritz or Tante

Marlene. "You didn't tell me your friends are Germans," she said to Jill.

"Does it matter?"

"And who is Claire?" asked Mrs. Parsons, ignoring Jill's question.

"A Wren we met on the train. I told my mother we'd be with her."

"Excuse me." Tante Marlene stepped forward and took a deep breath. Her bosom rose under the ruffles on her blouse. "I see the children spent the night with you, Mrs. Parsons, and I thank you for taking care of them. Their mother is waiting now in Cambridge. So we must go."

"How can I be sure these children are safe with you?" Mrs. Parsons stood between Jill and Tante Marlene. Jill stared at Mrs. Parsons.

Jill moved around Mrs. Parsons and slipped her hand into Tante Marlene's. "Tante Marlene's husband works at the clinic with my father and Fritz is an air raid patrol warden who knows about air raid safety. We'll be fine, thank you."

"And Fritz lives with us so he knows the way home," said Enid, patting Fritz's arm.

"I drive many times from London to Cambridge, Mrs. Parsons, and I know very well the journey," said Tante Marlene evenly.

Jill wondered how Tante Marlene could be so calm and composed in the face of Mrs. Parsons's anger. She remembered how even Claire had reacted badly when she'd learned Jill's friends were Germans. How many times did Tante Marlene and Fritz have to defend themselves for being German?

Mrs. Parsons folded her arms and set her mouth in a line and Jill prepared herself for an argument but Mrs. Parsons stepped back.

"Well, you better go. Your mother is waiting for you. Just be careful."

Fritz hoisted Enid and Tuppence onto his shoulders and Enid balanced Tuppence on Fritz's head.

"He better not pee on me."

Hattie reached up her chubby arms.

"Tuppi stay," she said.

"Sorry, Hattie," said Enid. "But he has to go with me. You can come and visit him if you like."

Lewis reached into his school bag and took out his book on reptiles.

"Here, Enid. You can have this."

"Thanks, Lewis!" Enid took the book and hugged it to her chest.

As they turned to go, Lewis discreetly tucked a piece of folded paper into Jill's hand. Jill turned pink.

"Bye, Lewis," she said, slipping the note in her pocket.

A few people watched them walk to the exit. When they climbed the stairs, they heard the flat tone of the "all clear" whistle.

Above ground, plaster dust filled the air, catching in Jill's throat and making her cough. She stared at the space where she and Enid had waited the day before and she let out a gasp. Shattered glass from the roof canopy and lumps of twisted metal littered the ground. The burnt out remains of several passenger carriages lay beyond the platform gates where their train had pulled in from Bletchley yesterday. She wondered what had happened to the passengers. She could easily have been one of them.

Outside the station, layers of dust blocked the sunlight and blurred the skyline into a smoky haze.

"Should we wear our gas masks?" Jill noticed that few people in London carried their masks.

"There is no poisonous gas," said Fritz.

"But my eyes hurt," Enid cried, rubbing at them with her fists.

"Tie this over your eyes, liebchen." Tante Marlene passed a handkerchief up to Enid and she held it to her eyes. "Soon we reach the car."

A man in a bowler hat emerged from the smoke, using his rolled umbrella as a walking stick.

"We're down, but we're not out," he said as he went by.

"What's he talking about?" asked Enid.

"That London is hurt, but still she fights," said Fritz.

An ambulance moved slowly through the rubble.

Everywhere she looked, Jill saw the ragged remains of buildings spilling out onto the street. Those left standing had dark glassless windows. A woman hung out of one and threw bundles of clothing to some children below.

Several rescue workers shoveled bricks from

damaged shops. A line formed outside a bakery named *Baileys*. The glass in its windows was gone as well but a sign read "Open For Business". The joke caught Jill by surprise. She'd heard how brave Londoners were in the midst of bombings and now she could see it was true.

The roof of the shop next door was missing. A man and woman piled furniture out on the sidewalk while a white-faced boy sat on a broken chair, talking to a parakeet in a cage.

"We have to stop for just a minute," said Enid.

She climbed down from Fritz's shoulders so she could get closer look.

"He's just like Peter's parakeet, isn't he, Jill?"

"Yes, he is." Jill's thoughts ran from Peter to Peter's dad, Eddie, lying injured in hospital, and to her father.

"Did Dad come home, Fritz?" she asked.

"No," said Fritz. "Not yet."

When Jill heard this, she forgot to be brave. The tears ran down her cheeks. Fritz knelt down in front of her and made her look him in the eye.

"You cannot give up hope, Jill… ever."

"I'll try," said Jill.

She wiped the tears away. Fritz had never stopped hoping to be with Lonnie and now they were married and had Anna.

They continued on, weaving their way through crushed mortar and twisted metal.

"What is this stuff?" Enid reached down for a small

lump of metal on the street.

"Shrapnel," said Tante Marlene. "A piece of exploded bomb."

"Cripes." Enid dropped the metal as if it was still hot, but Jill retrieved it.

When she got back to Cambridge a piece of shrapnel would remind her that she really had been to London, and London would remind her of Lewis.

"Look at all this silver paper." Enid kicked at the shiny scraps scattered over the ground.

"It's tin foil. They scatter it to garble German radar signals," said Fritz.

Tante Marlene pointed to the next corner.

"The car is around there," she said.

When Tante Marlene unlocked the car doors Jill climbed into the back seat next to Enid. She leaned into the soft leather. The smell reminded her of the chairs in her father's clinic.

Tante Marlene slid into the car and reached for a paper bag.

"I have in here some apple strudel and some penguin biscuits."

"Thank you, but no," said Jill, not feeling hungry. Usually she loved Tante Marlene's strudel but today the smell of apples reminded her of her mother's pies on Sunday, with her father sitting next to her at the kitchen table.

Enid reached for a penguin biscuit. She unwrapped

the foil-covered chocolate wafers, sandwiched together with chocolate cream, and ate every crumb, smiling contentedly and slowly stroking Tuppence's shell.

Tante Marlene started up the car and joined the thin stream of traffic moving slowly down the centre of the street.

"I follow the cars and hope we find a way out of London," she said, squinting ahead through the window.

Jill watched Enid flatten the empty foil from her penguin biscuit until the penguin picture on it was smooth and shiny.

"What happened to Claire?" asked Fritz. "We should phone but the telephone lines they are down."

"When Enid and I got through the ticket barrier at St. James's Park, she disappeared."

"This disappearment, it is strange," said Fritz.

"Where she worked at Bletchley is strange, too. She couldn't talk about it at all."

"Top secret, eh?" said Fritz.

"I thought a man was following us all the way from Bletchley to London, but he could have been following Claire."

"You trust her, this Claire?" asked Tante Marlene.

"Yes," said Jill. "You would have, too. She's a Wren and her mother lives in London."

Tante Marlene concentrated on the road, her lips pressed around her tortoiseshell cigarette holder. Gripping the steering wheel, she maneuvered the car around the edge of a hole the size of a double-decker bus. A large sign said "Keep Back, Explosives". At the bottom of the hole a group of men huddled over what Jill thought must be a bomb. Chunks of broken pavement lay scattered around like giant cake crumbs. A fire truck blocked the way ahead and Tante Marlene threw up her hands.

"Mensch! Müssen Wir hier bis Mittwoch warten?" Her cigarette wiggled as she spoke.

"You're talking German, Tante Marlene," Enid giggled.

"I complain better in German." Tante Marlene flashed a tight-lipped smile. Ash from her cigarette dropped into her lap. Fritz shook his finger.

"Always you burn holes in your dresses."

Enid giggled again and Jill felt relieved that even though they were in the middle of London, the morning after a bomb attack, her sister seemed almost content.

Tante Marlene backed up and detoured through a side street, where she competed with a horse-drawn wagon piled high with furniture. The constant scream of sirens told Jill that many people had been injured or killed in last night's attack. She was glad when they left the city streets and made their way through the suburbs north of London. On every street corner she saw anti-aircraft machine guns just like the ones in Cambridge.

They passed beyond all the houses and the road continued north through the fields to Harlow. When they reached a big intersection, a pile of rusted out vehicles blocked the road. Tante Marlene turned onto a side road.

"Why is the main road blocked?" asked Jill.

"They are worried about fifth columnists hiding in the countryside," said Fritz.

"Lots of them?" Enid looked anxiously out of the window.

"Nobody knows, but don't worry Enid." Fritz winked. "I'll save you."

Jill got tired of looking out of the window and tried to distract herself by making up a poem:

> "If we can make it through this war
> I'll make my bed and wash the floor,
> Send all my savings to the poor
> And offer help from door to door
> And get along with Enid more...."

Jill stopped herself. The poem was ridiculous, like a list of New Year's resolutions she'd never keep. She watched Enid offer leftover strudel to Tuppence but he wouldn't eat. Then Enid opened the reptile book from Lewis. Jill reached into her pocket and felt the edges of the note from him. When she was alone, she'd read it.

In Bishop's Stortford there was another barricade. When the car drew close, a group of Home Guardsmen in brown uniforms and dark green tin hats picked up their rifles. One of them stepped forward and signaled at Tante Marlene to stop.

"Whatever do they want?" Tante Marlene sounded

irritated.

"I don't know." Fritz looked pale.

"Everybody out of the car – hurry up now. We haven't got all day," said the guardsman abruptly.

Enid hesitated.

"Tuppence is asleep," she said, looking at Jill with big frightened eyes.

"He'll be fine." Jill took her hand. "And so will you," she whispered. "Come on, Een."

Outside the air smelled fresh and green. Jill watched the guardsmen check the trunk, the glove compartment, under and down between the seats. He even made them open their gas mask boxes.

"Nothing here," he said.

Jill was very glad she'd given the pamphlets to Claire at King's Cross station.

"Let's have your names, where you came from and where you're going." The guard propped his rifle against the barricade and took out a notebook. When Fritz spoke, the guard looked up in surprise.

"You're a bloody German."

Jill shifted from one foot to the other, anxiously waiting for Fritz to answer.

"Yes, I am German," said Fritz. "I live in England since before the war began."

"He is my brother," said Tante Marlene. "And..."

"And you came over here together," interrupted the guard.

"No, I live here. My husband Harry is English. Fritz lives with Harry's partner, Tom Richards. We invited Fritz to England so he could escape from the Nazis."

"Hmm," said the guard. "Another one of those refugees. What do you Germans think this country is, eh? A bloody vacation resort?"

His helmet strap cut into his pink cheeks and beads of sweat trickled down his forehead. He turned towards Jill.

"I suppose you're a bloody German too, eh?"

Fritz stepped forward. "Please do not speak with her like that. She is Tom Richards's daughter. I live at her house."

Jill explained how she and Enid had taken a wrong train and that Fritz and Tante Marlene had come down to London to take them home.

When the guard spoke to Enid she tried to hide behind Tante Marlene.

"What do you have to say, young lady?"

"I… I didn't want to go to Bletchley or to London," Enid stammered. "I… I want to go home."

Jill thought the guard frowned when he heard Bletchley. He motioned Fritz forward.

"I'd better see your papers."

He escorted Fritz to a makeshift desk.

"What are they doing?" whispered Enid.

"They check Fritz's visa and passport and also his internment release paper. Always they check papers

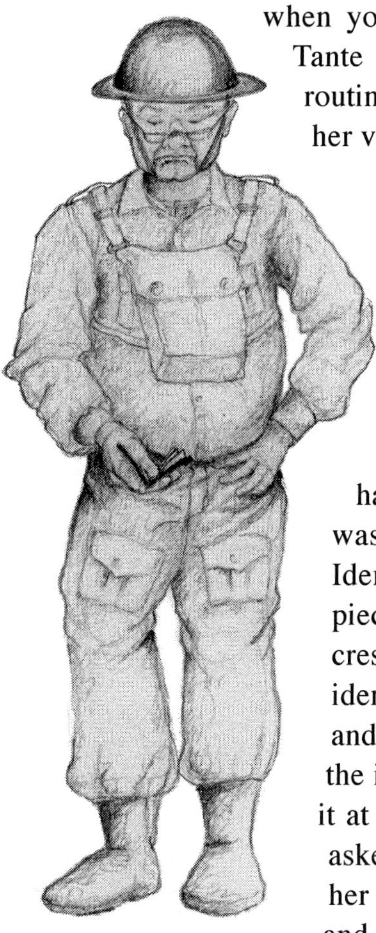

when you speak with an accent." Tante Marlene made this sound routine but Jill heard anger in her voice.

Jill watched the guard take out a pair of reading glasses and thumb through Fritz's passport, stopping to study his visa page. She wondered what would have happened if he hadn't had it with him. All Jill had was a National Registration Identity Card, a small folded piece of cardstock with a royal crest on the outside, her name, identification number, address, and her father's signature on the inside. But her mother had it at home. What if the guards asked for it now? Jill slipped her arm into Tante Marlene's and whispered, "Mum has our identification cards."

"Don't worry, liebchen." Tante Marlene patted Jill's hand.

"So," said the guard, looking at Fritz over the top

of his reading glasses. "It says here you were interned on the Isle of Man, May 10, 1940, to March 3, 1941. Let you out two months ago, eh?"

"Yes," said Fritz quietly.

"I see they rejected you as a pioneer."

Fritz looked at his feet.

"I do not have useful qualifications for a war," said Fritz.

"Maybe you've just become useful."

"What do you mean?" asked Fritz.

"We're looking for someone," said the guard, pulling a notepad from his pocket and checking the details. "I'm taking you to headquarters for further questioning. You might be him."

"Whatever you are thinking, you are mistaken." Fritz's neck flushed as red as his hair. "I come to London only to take the children home."

Tante Marlene stepped forward.

"I can't let you take him." Her voice was icy cold. "He is a good man, my brother. He has done nothing wrong. He works hard for his family and for this country."

"That's what they all say, lady." The guard pulled out a set of handcuffs and grabbed Fritz by the wrist. "Let's just say," he sneered, "that he is innocent until proven guilty."

Jill watched in horror as the handcuffs clicked shut. This couldn't be happening, not to Fritz! She clenched her hands, set her shoulders and stepped in front of the guard.

"I know who you're looking for – these two men who… "

She didn't get any further. Tires squealed behind them and a lorry sped into view. It slowed briefly, then picked up speed and smashed right through the barricade. Jill turned just in time to read the license plate. She jumped out of the way as a guard raised his rifle and shot at the lorry tires. Enid screamed. When the lorry didn't stop, two guards clambered into a jeep and raced after it.

"It's them!" Jill yelled at the guard. "That's the lorry you're looking for.

Chapter 10

Jill watched the familiar lorry disappear down the road, the jeep chasing after it. She wanted to chase it, too.

"That's the lorry Enid and I got stuck in," Jill yelled to Tante Marlene. "The one that took us to Bletchley."

The guard who had asked all the questions pulled out a large handkerchief and mopped his brow. A dark circle of sweat spread down from his armpit. He wasn't a young man and Jill thought that out here in the countryside, his daily routine didn't usually include car chases and spy interrogations. When he finished dabbing at his forehead he called out to the guard who had fired the shots.

"Put your rifle down, mate, and radio the next blockade." He turned to Jill. "Where were we?" he asked looking at her over the top of his glasses, without his former hostility. "Ah yes – the lorry."

He listened attentively while Jill told how she and Enid had ended up in the back of the lorry, about the parachute in the woods, the mysterious machine with typewriter keys, being taken to Bletchley and about how they had escaped.

"Could you identify the men in the lorry?" asked the guard.

"No," said Jill. "But I think one of them was on the train to London. When we got to London he followed us to St. James's Park on the underground train."

"He took Claire," whispered Enid, poking her head from behind Tante Marlene's where she had been hiding.

"We think he kidnapped our friend Claire," explained Jill.

"I don't suppose you saw the lorry's license plate," said the guard.

"Yes, I did."

The guard smiled as he wrote down the letters and numbers in his notebook. Then he scribbled something on a piece of paper and gave it to Tante Marlene.

"You're free to go. Show this if you're stopped again." He turned to Fritz. "Sorry about the misunderstanding... sir. Just doing my duty, that's all." He unlocked the handcuffs and tipped his hat. "Good luck to you, sir."

They got in the car and Enid picked Tuppence off the back seat and set him on her lap. No one spoke as Tante Marlene drove through the broken barricade. Even

Enid stayed quiet for a while, her face pressed against the leather seat and her eyes moving slowly from Fritz to Tante Marlene. Jill saw smudges of dirt on Enid's cheeks, streaked clean where tears had trickled. She reached over and squeezed her sister's arm.

"We'll be home soon, Een."

Enid nodded, running her fingers lovingly around the small geometric plates that formed Tuppence's shell. Tuppence poked out his head and Enid kissed the top of it.

"That's disgusting, Een."

"No it's not. He smells of straw and the garden shed at home."

For a while, Enid sat with her eyes closed and Tuppence tucked into her arms. Then she opened her eyes and sat up. "Fritz?"

"Yes?"

"Were you afraid at the barricade?"

"A bit, but mostly angry. Always I have to answer questions because I am German."

"Tuppence should have taken a bite out of that guard with his powerful jaws."

Enid ran her finger along the jagged line of Tuppence's mouth and Jill expected a speech about the sharp hooks he used to tear at his food, but apparently Enid had more questions. "Fritz?"

"Yes?"

"When the guard looked at your papers, he said

you were rejected as a pioneer. What's a pioneer?"

"It is a group who digs ditches and builds bunkers. I

couldn't be one because they already had too many."

"Did you really want to dig ditches?"

"No. But I really wanted to be released from the camp. The men and women who were useful got released sooner – vegetable gardeners, scientists, doctors, nurses – people like that. But I had no qualifications so I had to stay until the government decided I was not a spy."

"Why don't you have qualifications?" asked Enid innocently.

"Because I am studying at the university in Berlin when the Nazis make all the Jewish professors leave so there are no more teachers."

Enid fell silent for a minute and then she said, "I hope I'll have professors to teach me how to be a veterinarian."

"I'm sure you will," said Fritz. "The war will be over by the time you go to university."

Jill sat thinking about Fritz being held on the Isle of Man. She knew Lonnie hadn't had to go because she was pregnant with Anna.

"Fritz... did women have to be interned?"

"Yes," said Fritz. "If Lonnie had to come, we couldn't have been together. The women and children stayed in different camps from the men."

"You must have missed Lonnie while you were gone," said Jill.

"Yes, very much. When they wanted to put me on a ship to Canada I thought I'd never see Lonnie again.

Then Anna was born and I can stay – because I became the father of a British child. I am lucky, yes?"

"Yes," said Enid.

Jill hadn't known that Anna's birth gave Fritz the right to be in England, and how narrowly he had escaped being sent to Canada.

"I am lucky twice," said Fritz. "The ship I would have sailed on to Canada, it was torpedoed by a U-boat and sank."

Jill winced at the thought of Lonnie without a husband and Anna without a father. How could Fritz be so cheerful in spite of all that?

"Do you still feel lucky that you came to England?" asked Jill.

"Yes," said Fritz, without hesitation. "I marry Lonnie, I have Anna. Those are my dearest wishes. *And* I don't have to be a Nazi."

Jill decided she wanted to be more like Fritz. He knew how to make choices, while she had difficulty deciding how many cabbages to grow in her Victory Garden.

"Where are we now?" Enid pressed her nose so close to the window that condensation formed around it.

"We're close to Saffron Walden," said Tante Marlene.

"How do you know? I haven't seen any signs," said Enid.

"There aren't any," said Jill. "Mum said they took

them all down after the war began."

"So we'd all get lost?"

"No, silly. So fifth columnists would get lost."

"But spies have maps, don't they? There was a map in the lorry."

Jill couldn't deny this.

"Well, maybe the government hopes they'll lose their maps."

"Do you think we'll see the lorry again?" asked Enid.

"Not if the jeep caught up with it," said Tante Marlene.

Jill must have dozed because suddenly they were on Trumpington Road, entering Cambridge, with the trees and grass of Grantchester Meadows stretching away on her right. The spires of Cambridge came into view, soaring skyward. They neared the university colleges, where a few student cyclists hugged the curbs. Jill relaxed a little. Cambridge seemed very peaceful after the clamour of London. When they reached their street, Toots, the neighbor's black cat, ran along the sidewalk and hid under a hedge. Then they were home.

Mum opened the door and Jill ran up the path into her arms.

"Thank goodness you're safe!" she said.

Jill looked up at her mother's face and saw dark rings around her eyes. She wore yesterday's clothes and Jill knew she'd sat up all night worrying.

"Is Dad here?"

"No," said Mum. "When they'd cleared the rubble at the bomb site, there was no sign of your father."

Chapter 11

Jill followed her mother into the house. Lonnie came out of her room looking pale and worried. She gave Fritz a big hug.

"Steve is making search plans at his house," Mum stated.

"I'll go back out to help find Tom," said Fritz.

"Thank you," she replied.

When Fritz had gone Tante Marlene put on the kettle. Enid told Mum how frightened Tuppence had been.

"It was dark and smelly in the lorry and he wouldn't come out of his shell and when we ran away in Bletchley, I dropped him on the pavement and broke a scute." The words tumbled out.

Mum examined the broken shell.

"It'll grow it back, won't it, dear?"

But Enid had other things on her mind. "Guess who we saw in London, Mum."

"Who?"

"Charles," said Enid.

Mum looked surprised.

"And he knows Claire," said Jill. "Charles works in the London office with her. He wanted to help us but he had other stuff to do."

"I bet you wish he'd taken us home," said Enid. Jill turned bright red.

"Shut up, Een." Now they were home, Enid was being her usual pesky self.

"I can say what I like," said Enid rudely.

Jill decided to change the subject.

"Claire was really kind, Mum. She works in Bletchley and when we showed her the codebooks we'd found in the lorry, she said they were top secret and we had to take them to the War Office in London. It was on the way to the War Office that Claire disappeared, so we went back to King's Cross station and this lady named Mrs. Parsons invited us to join her family on the underground platform until Fritz and Tante Marlene came."

"And people slept on the underground platform but it was so noisy," said Enid, "and Hattie wanted to hold Tuppence, but I only let her touch him gently and Jill went off with Hattie's brother, didn't you Jill?" Enid gave Jill a knowing look. "Then on the way home the guard shot his rifle at the barricade and Tuppence thought he'd die and…."

Mum listened with increasing concern until Enid had finished.

"I'm proud of you both," she said, hugging Jill and Enid close.

"I'm going outside," announced Enid. "Tuppence is very, very tired and he wants to sleep in the shed and dream celestial dreams."

Feeling unsettled, Jill ate some lunch then hung around in the kitchen while her mother went out to get the washing off the line. Lonnie came in and sat Anna in her high chair. Jill buttered a slice of bread for her, cut it into strips and bounced one towards Anna's mouth. "Here come the soldiers marching into your mouth."

Anna bit a piece off one end.

"There goes his head," said Jill.

Anna let out a delighted whoop. She squeezed the rest of the bread strip into a greasy pulp. Gooey mush spread through her fingers and soon, soggy breadcrumbs littered the high chair tray and the floor below. Lonnie cleaned them up and kissed the top of Anna's head.

"I'm kissing the cleanest part of you, Anna," she said cheerfully, then turned to Jill. "How are you, Jill, after all your excitements?"

"I'm worried sick about Dad," Jill confessed. "If Dad wasn't at Eddie's house, where is he? How can they be sure he isn't under the rubble?" Jill imagined her father buried under chunks of broken concrete, hit by a stray bomb on his way to the fire or lying injured in the woods. He must be hurt, or he would have phoned. "Fritz told me I can't give up hope."

"Many times he tells me that too, when he is in prison in Berlin, when we try to get out of Germany, when he is taken away to internment camp – always he says to keep hoping."

"I wish I was brave like you, Lonnie."

"You are, Jill. You kept Enid safe until Fritz and Marlene bring you both home."

When Lonnie took Anna to the bathroom to wipe her face, Jill slipped outside and walked across the patio.

Dandelions pushed up through the paving stones. The yellow blooms shone like melted butter in the morning sun. Beyond the patio, rows of green shoots ran through the dirt in Jill's victory garden – peas, beans and carrots. Jill took the shrapnel out of her pocket and set it by a row of carrots, then she walked down the path through the grass to the shed. She could hear Enid talking to Tuppence.

Jill poked her head around the door. Tuppence was

in his box under a pile of straw.

"Tuppence is dreaming that Dad came back," said Enid.

"Dreams do come true. If you need me Een, I'm up in my tree."

A pair of apple trees stood near the shed. Fresh white blossoms covered the branches, promising a rich crop of apples in the fall. Jill stepped into the fork of her favourite tree and as she climbed, she heard Mr. Reid's chickens scratching in the dirt next door. Last summer her mother had made her trade carrots and peas for a chicken dinner. She couldn't watch when Mr. Reid wrung the chicken's neck. Now he had three chubby piglets, soon to become pork chops and rashers of bacon.

Balancing on her usual branch, Jill pressed her nose into the blossoms. Then she pulled Lewis's note from her pocket and opened it. In neat script were the words, "Please write to Lewis Parsons, 14 Argyle Square, London." Jill smiled, folded the note and put it back in her pocket. She would write when her father came home.

Being up in the tree helped Jill think things out. "Dad thinks while he digs in the garden. I think up here," she said to herself. She imagined her father's face looking up at her through the apple blossoms. When she was seven he'd helped her learn to hang upside down from her branch, standing below her to catch her if she fell.

Jill mulled over the events of the last twenty-four hours. She thought about the bush in the woods where she'd discovered the parachute. While crawling around it, looking for Tuppence, she had noticed an unusual amount of broken branches. Hiding a parachute couldn't have broken that many. Then she remembered. Her father had said they'd check the woods when she'd told him about the plane she'd seen above the trees. Maybe he couldn't wait to see and had gone through the woods on his way to the firehouse. Something could have happened. Jill dropped backwards and somersaulted neatly from the branch to the ground.

"Een," she said, poking her head into the shed. "I'm riding over to the woods."

"Wait. I'll come too." Enid stuffed Tuppence's old straw into the compost bin and grabbed her bike. "I'll keep up, I promise."

When they opened the back gate, Fritz came walking up the lane.

"I thought you were out looking for Dad," said Jill.

"Yes, but I need my bike. Where are you two going?"

"To the woods," said Enid.

"To look for Dad," said Jill.

"Why the woods?"

"Remember the parachute?" said Jill. "Dad may have gone to check it out. He often walked through the woods on his way to the fire hall." Fritz's eyes lit up.

"I'll ride with you."

The midday sun shone high above them as they rode down the lane to the road and where the trees began. Entering the woods felt like walking into the grey vaulted space of Christ's College chapel. The trees formed an arch above their heads, shading the path ahead.

The air smelled damp and loamy. Buds pushed up through the rhododendron leaves and beneath them, a robin pecked at the dirt.

"When we come here with Dad," said Jill, "he likes to go adventuring down every narrow trail. 'Think about all you're missing if you stay on the path,' he says. He always finds the first crocus in February and the first bird's nest in March."

Jill, Enid and Fritz got off their bikes and looked around. Two red squirrels chased each other up the trunk of a horse chestnut tree.

"Here we are." Jill pointed to her right. "This is where we left the path and lost Tuppence."

"I hate going in there," said Enid. "It's spooky."

"Do not worry." Fritz beat on his chest like an earth bound Tarzan. "I am here."

Enid grinned as they left the path and squeezed

through the rhododendron branches. Fritz slapped at his arms.

"Biting bugs! Just like in the woods at Zeuthen."

"Where's Zeuthen?" asked Enid, ducking under a leafy branch.

"Near Berlin. My family had a summer cottage by a lake."

"Ooh, lucky you. Did you go swimming?"

"Sometimes," said Fritz. "We had a rowboat and my friend Lucas, he tells me to row between the tall rushes and we see a grey heron sitting on her nest. And," Fritz paused to grin, "we used to make beer in the cottage cellar and never told my mother."

"Is Lucas still your friend?"

"I don't know," said Fritz, looking into the bushes. "He joined the army and became a Nazi."

"How do you know?" asked Enid.

"He told me before I left."

It was bad enough having Emily White call her a "Nazi lover" but to have your best friend become one would be terrible. "He didn't have to, did he?" asked Jill.

"I like to think he had no choice."

"Here we are," said Jill pushing through the bushes to where she had found the parachute. Now the area was flattened and broken branches covered the ground.

“Wow,” said Fritz looking around. “What happened?”

“I think there was a fight.” Jill reached down and poked in the dirt. “What’s this?”

“It’s something disgusting, that’s what it is,” said Enid.

“No it’s not, Een. Look. It’s a handkerchief.”

Jill held up the muddy piece of cloth.

“Eeeu!” Enid held her nose. “Mum would tell you not to touch someone else’s snotty old handkerchief.”

Instinctively, Jill dropped the handkerchief, but Fritz picked it up.

“Look,” he said pulling out a corner. “There are some initials.”

Jill saw the letters “TR”.

“‘TR’? Tom Richards! It’s Dad’s!” said Jill. “Dad was here. He must have bumped into the spies. We have to go home and tell Mum.”

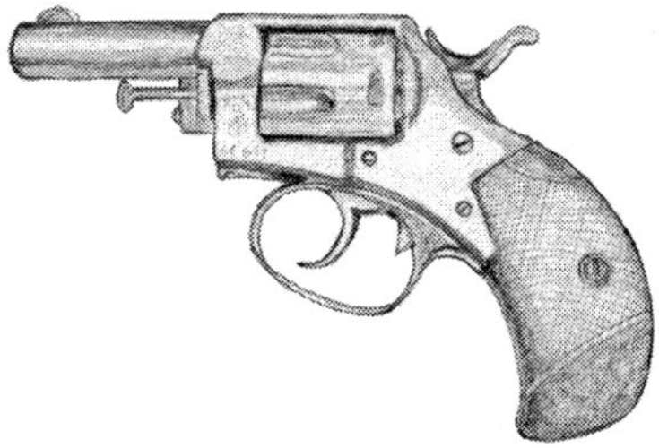

Chapter 12

Steve, the fire chief, was sitting at the kitchen table with Mum when Jill, Enid and Fritz walked in the back door. He rubbed his temples as he stared down into a cup of tea. Jill could tell that he was exhausted.

"Mum," she said softly. "Look what we found in the woods."

She held up her father's handkerchief.

"It's Dad's handkerchief," said Enid, ducking under Jill's arm and pushing her way forward. "Jill found it and Fritz saw Dad's initials in the corner."

"There was a scuffle in the woods," said Fritz. "And…"

"And the spies took Dad," interrupted Enid. "Steve, you wouldn't believe all the things that have happened to us since we last saw you."

Mum pulled up two chairs.

"Why don't you both sit down and tell Steve everything?"

Half an hour later, Steve had heard about a parachute in the woods, spies driving Jill and Enid to Bletchley Park, strange looking typewriters, Claire's disappearance and a night in the London underground station. He sat back in his chair and blinked.

"When we came home we heard that Dad wasn't at Eddie's house," said Jill, "Then I thought he might have gone through the woods and something happened to him before he reached the firehall."

"He bumped into the spies, right?" said Steve.

"Yes, I think so," said Jill.

Steve considered this and turned to Mum.

"If it's alright with you, Peggy, we can organize a search party."

Mum nodded.

"Can I help?" asked Jill. "Please?"

"No," said Mum quickly. "I need you around here."

Steve and Fritz left. There was nothing to do but wait so Jill did chores. She vacuumed all the carpets. When she came to Lonnie and Fritz's room, Anna crawled behind her, making "vooming" noises. Jill dusted the windowsills, being careful not to break her mother's favourite Chinese vase. While she worked, she promised herself that if her father came home safely, she'd do chores for the rest of her life.

Where had he been taken? Down to London or even to a prison camp in Germany, like Claire's father? Was Claire being questioned roughly in some small, dark room? Would Charles be safe getting out of London when he'd finished his work? She shuddered at these thoughts as she dusted the rows of medical texts and journals on her father's bookshelf. When she'd shined the shelves, she helped Lonnie and her mother fold the wash.

Mum handed Jill a pile of shirts, pajamas and underwear. "Here. This batch goes up to Charles's room."

Her arms stacked with clothing, Jill climbed the stairs and pushed Charles's door open with her foot. Usually he was home and took his clothes from her at the door. Jill liked it when he smiled at her and said, "Thank you." Since he wasn't there, she walked in and dumped them on his bed.

Jill felt strange in this room. Before the war, it had been the study, a cozy and welcoming room with its large desk nestled into the window, the sofa draped with her parents' old bedspread to cover the holes, and some of her favourite books on the shelves. But Charles had needed a room when he came to teach mathematics at the university so her parents had rented it to him. Now it looked different, with Charles's stuff spread everywhere. Clothes, books and old newspapers covered the chairs and spilled onto the floor. Dark portraits of serious-looking men, maybe mathematicians, hung from the walls. Their penetrating eyes stared back at Jill. Charles kept his heavy blackout curtains half drawn. Jill thought she saw one of the curtains move and made herself look behind it. But it was only a breeze through the open window.

She had turned to leave when she noticed a case tucked under Charles's bed. Its size and shape reminded her of the one in the lorry. Jill dropped to her knees to get a closer look. She didn't usually pry, but she had to see what was inside. She pulled the case out onto the carpet, hoping it wasn't locked. The latches clicked, the lid opened and Jill stared at the machine inside.

Three rows of push buttons arranged like typewriter keys held the letters of the alphabet. Behind these, three more rows of a second alphabet appeared in circles on a board. Above the board, four cog-like wheels were marked with four more alphabets. Jill remembered the diagram in the pamphlet she had given Claire. This was the same machine.

Why did Charles have a machine like this hidden under his bed and why had he been in London yesterday, when he'd said he was working at the university? It must be connected to the top secret stuff Claire said she couldn't talk about.

Leaving the machine open on the floor, Jill turned to Charles's messy desk. One side was piled high with textbooks. On the other side, a metal tray held papers, and Jill thought they must be student tests. In the middle of the desk lay an ink-stained blotter, with notes sticking

out of the sides.

Feeling like a spy, Jill glanced at the door and listened. There was no sound on the landing. Her palms felt sweaty as she reached towards the desk and pulled one of the notes out from under the blotter. Random letters had been scribbled across it and below them other letters had been grouped to form strange words – German words.

A photo half under the blotter caught her eye. She pulled it out and the pit of her stomach churned. She recognized the face immediately. It was the man on the train from Bletchley. "Horst Reiter" read the name under the picture.

Why did Charles have a photo of a spy? Was he a government agent tracking down spies? Was that the secret work he and Claire did in London? She reached forward to push the photo under the blotter.

"I'll have that," said a voice behind her.

Jill dropped the picture and turned to face Charles.

"I… I'm sorry Charles." Jill stumbled backwards over a book on the floor. "I shouldn't be looking at your stuff. I brought up your washing and I…"

But Charles hardly seemed to notice her. He walked over to the opened machine, slammed the lid down and set it by the bedroom door. While Jill stood speechless, he swung a small suitcase off the top of the wardrobe and began jamming books and clothes into it. He stopped for a minute to pull the curtain back and glance down into the street.

"Bloody hell," said Charles. The front door opened and footsteps sounded on the stairs. "It's your damned fault… you stupid, interfering girl! You and your damned father!"

Grabbing Jill around the neck, he pushed her roughly towards the door. She felt something cold pressing into the side of her neck.

"What's going on in there?" Jill heard her mother call.

"Come any further and I'll shoot her!" Charles yelled at the door.

Had Charles gone mad? Why was he doing this to her? He tightened his grip on Jill's neck and the buttons on his jacket sleeve pressed into her throat until she could barely breathe. She lost her balance and her heels scuffed along the carpet as Charles dragged her, like a rag doll, behind the bedroom door.

"You're surrounded, Charles. Just drop the gun," said Claire's voice.

There was a crash at the window. Glass shattered and Charles spun around. Jill felt herself pushed forcefully aside. Her head cracked against the wall and everything turned black.

Chapter 13

Jill opened her eyes and saw her father's face.

"Dad!" She reached up to hug him and winced as a sharp pain shot through her head.

Dad bent down and kissed her.

"Lie still, dear. You got a nasty gash when you cracked your head against the wall in Charles's room."

Jill saw that she was lying on her parents' bed in the dining room. Then she remembered being in Charles's room with cold gunmetal pressed into her neck. Tears filled her eyes and ran down the sides of her face onto the pillow.

"Don't cry, dear." When Dad wiped away her tears Jill saw welts on her father's wrists. She brushed her fingers across the marks.

"You're hurt, Dad."

"My battle scars," said Dad. "You were right about me going through the woods on Friday. I bumped into Charles gathering up the parachute. He and his accomplice weren't too pleased to see me. They tied me up and locked me in a shed on the other side of the woods."

"Charles locked you up?"

"Yes," said Dad. "Steve and Fritz found me just a little while ago, thanks to your quick thinking."

Jill managed a small smile.

"I was so worried about you, Dad," she whispered. "I thought you might be dead." She took in her father's face, eyes hollow from lack of sleep. He gave her a long hug.

"And now, if you're up for it, there's someone else to see you."

"Who?"

"You'll see."

Dad disappeared into the hall. Seconds later, Claire came through the door.

"Claire," said Jill, "you're here!"

"Yes, I am." Claire knelt by the bed and rested her arms on the covers. She looked exhausted like Dad, and her Wren uniform was all crumpled.

"Are you all right?" asked Jill.

"I am now," said Claire. "But I let you and Enid down. One minute I was looking for train tickets in my purse and the next thing I knew, I was lying flat on my back in a first aid station. They said I fainted, too much work and too little sleep or something. When they let me go, I couldn't find you anywhere."

Enid came in and sat on the end of the bed.

"I was wrong," she said. "Spies didn't get her after all."

"There was nothing to do," continued Claire, "but go to the War Office. I told Charles what had happened and he went to find you. When he came back he said not to worry. He'd put you on the train to Cambridge. Then the air raid siren went off and I had to spend the night in the War Office basement. Early this morning, I saw Charles leave the office and that's when I knew."

"Knew what?" asked Jill.

"That Charles was up to something. He wasn't driving his Morris Minor. He was in a lorry with Horst Reiter. The registration number was JTE 143, the number on the lorry that took you to Bletchley."

"So Charles was in that lorry?" Jill's eyes were wide.

"Yes," said Claire. "I couldn't catch him before he got here – and neither could the Home Guard. They told me that a smart young lady identified the lorry, but they lost track of it."

"Claire says Charles will go to prison," said Enid.

Jill expected Enid to ask how much Jill liked Charles now, but instead Enid said, "I'd hate to be in prison."

Thinking about Charles made Jill sad. She remembered how pleased she'd been when he appeared in the King's Cross Station café. And then she remembered something else that had happened in the café.

"Claire?" said Jill.

"Yes?"

"I meant to ask you..."

"Fire away," said Claire.

"That little black bag that fell out of your handbag – is it secret, too?"

Claire laughed.

"I always carry that. It holds a good luck charm my father gave me before he left for Germany."

"Oh," said Jill. She touched Claire's arm. "Will you write and tell me if…" Jill searched for words.

"If my father comes back… yes, of course I will," promised Claire, taking Enid's hand. "Now you rest. Enid said she'd take me down the yard to see where Tuppence lives."

Mum came in as Claire and Enid left. She pulled up a chair beside Jill.

"How are you, dear?" she asked, taking Jill's hand

in hers.

"O.K., I suppose. But Mum?"

"Yes, dear?"

"Why doesn't Charles want us to win the war?"

"I'm not sure," said Mum. "He once told me that, before the war began, he studied in Berlin. He said he liked it there and made lots of friends. When the war started, he said he stopped communicating with his German friends. Apparently that wasn't true."

Jill felt confused about Charles. She'd misjudged him and she thought she was good at judging people.

"I never suspected Charles." Jill's voice trembled.

"You couldn't have, dear. Don't be hard on yourself for liking him. We all did. And you're the one who always had faith in Fritz. That's more than I can say for myself. Speaking of Fritz," Mum added, "you probably don't remember this, but when Charles threatened you in his room, Fritz climbed up the drain pipe and smashed the window. When Charles turned to look, your father jumped on him."

A wide smile spread across Jill's face.

"Jill..."

"Yes, Mum?" Jill waited while her mother fiddled with the blankets.

"I was wrong about Fritz. I didn't trust him just because he was German and I'm sorry about that.

Your father and I have been talking," Mum continued. "Lonnie told us that Fritz is good with numbers. Well, Mrs. Hopkins is overworked at the clinic. If Fritz wants the job, he could be assistant accounts keeper at Christ's College. He'd make a lot more money than he does now."

"That's a great idea, Mum."

Jill relaxed back into the pillows. Yesterday her father had been missing and she and Enid were stranded on a London underground platform. And now she was safe at home with both her parents, making plans for Fritz. She couldn't ask for more. She'd write to Lewis today and tell him all about it.

Afterword

Bletchley Park is in Milton Keynes, just north of London. During World War II it became the headquarters of the British Government's Code and Cipher School. It is now a British "Historic Site", open to visitors.

The strange typewriter Jill saw was a German Enigma cipher machine, one of thousands used by the Germans and their allies to send coded messages during World War II. In February, 1940, four months after the war in Europe began, the crypto-analysts at Bletchley Park succeeded in breaking some of the codes. As the war progressed, the Nazis increased the complexity of the machines, but Britain, and later the United States, continued to break the codes.

The men and women who worked at Bletchley Park were sworn to secrecy and they were the only people to know that the codes were being broken. What happened at Bletchley Park remained Top Secret until thirty years after the war. Many experts now believe that deciphering the codes shortened the length of World War II.

Although the characters and plot are fictional, parts of this story are based on fact.

Lonnie and Fritz suffered the same prejudices and wartime hardships as my own parents, who fled Germany in 1939. Before leaving Germany, my father had been jailed by the Nazis for associating with my mother, who was half-Jewish. My parents looked to England for a better life. Upon their arrival they married in London and then moved to Cambridge when the war broke out. But as German refugees, they faced prejudice in their adopted country. The British Government, fearing that refugees would collaborate with German spies, sent my father and other Germans to an internment camp on the Isle of Man. He was held there, off the coast of Liverpool, for fourteen months. My mother was allowed to stay in Cambridge because she was pregnant. My sister was eight months old before my father was released.

As a teenager in England, I was embarrassed by my parents' German accents. When they went to school functions they didn't sound like all the other parents. Later in life I realized how their German accents must have made life difficult for them in England during the war and I have come to admire their courage.